Counselling
in
Terminal Care and
Bereavement

OTHER TITLES IN THE SERIES

Communication and Counselling in Health Care
Series editor: Hilton Davis

Counselling
in
Terminal Care and
Bereavement

Colin Murray Parkes
Consultant Psychiatrist to St Christopher's Hospice, Sydenham, & St
Joseph's Hospice, Hackney

Marilyn Relf
Manager, Bereavement Service, Sir Michael Sobell House, Oxford

Ann Couldrick
Bereavement Counsellor, Bereavement Service, Sir Michael Sobell House
& Counsellor in General Practice

Published by the British Psychological Society

First published in 1996 by BPS Books (The British Psychological Society),
St Andrews House, 48 Princess Road East, Leicester LEI 7DR.

Distributed exclusively in North America by Paul H. Brookes Publishing Co., Inc.,
P.O. Box 10624, Baltimore, Maryland 21285, USA.

A catalogue record for this book is available from the British Library

ISBN 1 85433 178 7

Origination by Ralph J. Footring, Derby
Printed in Great Britain by BPC Wheatons, Exeter

CONTENTS

Preface to the Series

People who suffer chronic disease or disability are confronted by problems that are as much psychological as physical, and involve all members of their family and the wider social network. Psychosocial adaptation is important in its own right, in terms of making necessary changes in life style, altering aspirations or coping with an uncertain future. However, it may also influence the effectiveness of the diagnostic and treatment processes, and hence eventual outcomes.

As a consequence, health care, whether preventive or treatment-orientated, must encompass the psychosocial aspects of illness as well as the physical, at all phases of the life cycle and at all stages of disease. The basis of this is skilled communication and supportive counselling by all involved in providing services, professionally or voluntarily. Everyone, from the student to the experienced practitioner, can benefit from appropriate training in this area, where the social skills required are complex and uncertain.

Although there is a sizeable research literature related to counselling and communication in the area of health care, specialist texts for training purposes are scarce. The current series was, therefore, conceived as a practical resource for all who work in health services. Each book is concerned with a specific area of health care. The authors have been asked to provide detailed information, from the patient's perspective, about the problems (physical, psychological and social) faced by patients and their families. Each book examines the role of counselling and communication in the process of helping people to come to terms and deal with these problems, and presents usable frameworks as a guide to the helping process. Detailed and practical descriptions of the major qualities, abilities and skills that are required to provide the most effective help for patients are included.

The intention is to stimulate professional and voluntary helpers alike to explore their efforts at supportive communication. It is hoped that by so doing, they become sufficiently aware of patient difficulties and the processes of adaptation, and more able to facilitate positive adjustment. The aims of the series will have been met if patients and their families feel someone has listened and if they feel respected in their struggle for health. A central theme is the effort to make people feel better about themselves and able to face the future, no matter how bleak, with dignity.

Hilton Davis
Series editor

Introduction

Peter Howick was dying. He knew it and the doctor knew it and sat there holding his hand and waiting. Peter was not in pain but was very weak and tired, drifting in and out of consciousness.

He had fought a long and courageous battle against cancer. He had cooperated well with the treatment and submitted uncomplainingly to several major surgical operations, but without success. His cancer had spread into his lungs and there was no longer any treatment which could be expected to prolong his life.

'It won't be long now,' he whispered. 'No, it won't be long,' the doctor replied, then added, gratuitously, 'You're not alone.' Peter gave him a long look. 'I am, you know,' he said.

And, of course, he was right. He was dying, not the doctor. As another patient said, 'It's like having a baby – you're the only one who can do it.' Yet dying is not usually a thing we choose to do: it happens to us. Peter was afraid, as we all must be when faced with the need to step into the unknown. In a sense he had died several times, for each time that he lost consciousness neither he nor the doctor knew whether he would awake again.

> 'This is the way the world ends,
> This is the way the world ends,
> This is the way the world ends,
> Not with a bang, but a whimper.'
>
> (Eliot, 1954, 'The Hollow Men')

Eventually Peter again drifted away and the doctor realized that, this time, he was not going to return. His breathing had changed from the regular stertor of the unconscious person to intermittent periods of shallow, automatic breathing alternating with periods of apnoea, in which he did not breathe at all. A little phlegm had accumulated in his chest, producing the so-called 'death rattle', but this was of no concern to Peter, who was deeply unconscious.

Death, when it came, was almost an anticlimax. The rattle stopped and the slight tension in his face ebbed away, leaving a reassuring look of serenity.

Peter's death was typical of the kind of death that takes place daily in hospitals, hospices and at home. In his case it happened to be a hospice. It was neither as wonderful as Pollyanna-like accounts of death in a hospice would lead one to expect, nor was it as horrific as the public image of death by cancer. Any pain that he might have suffered had been relieved, and, as a consequence of the illness, he had lost his appetites for food and for life itself. His only source of suffering was a kind of existential loneliness, a pervading sadness and apprehension. Old physicians termed this '*angor animi*', the acid test of faith.

Peter had no formal religious faith, and, even if he had, there is no reason to believe that it would have passed this particular test. What he did have was an impressive honesty and independence of mind that refused to cling to any sops of comfort that the doctor might throw to him. He chose to face his dying with objectivity and courage. By acknowledging the nature of his predicament he achieved a kind of heroism.

And the doctor, what did he make of this? I have to admit that Peter's death touched a very deep chord in me (CMP). His recognition of his own aloneness reminded me of Descartes' famous aphorism, 'I think, therefore I am'. But what if I can no longer think, what am I then? I wish I knew. We are all in the same boat, the only difference between the patient and me is the probability that he is going 'over the top' before I am. Clearly, I have a personal interest in the deaths of my patients and that must colour the way I react to them. A 'good death' reassures, a 'bad death' frightens me. It follows that those who look after the dying are also looking after themselves.

No matter how often it happens, death can never be taken for granted; it remains an awesome event for the patient, the family and the caring professions. In many instances it is easier to die than to survive. Patients may suffer fear and grief, but many of their fears can be alleviated, and those who choose to face the loss do not have to start again: their troubles will soon be over. For the family and others close to the patient it is very different. The death of a loved person is not only a loss, it is a turning point; the world will never be the same again. Each bereaved person faces a long period of adjustment to a life which is seldom wanted or planned.

As long as the patient is alive, his or her needs will come first: 'Don't you worry about us,' say the family, 'He's the one we must care for.' This is very right and proper; we must all look after the dying while we can, for there is nothing we can do for them when they are dead. But we should not imagine that this means that the family have no problems. It simply means that it may be difficult to help them with these problems while the patient lives.

Once death has occurred, the situation usually changes. Now the nearest and dearest can acknowledge their own needs, and they often go through a period of psychological distress that is far greater than the sufferings of the dying. Their grief is a reflection of their attachment to the one who has died, and to understand one we must understand the other.

From the moment of our birth we are accumulating experiences that will colour the way each of us perceives and responds to the world. The attachments that we make in childhood cause us to modify these perceptions and response tendencies. The people we love become tangled up with us in a network of unique interlocking systems of thought and behaviour, which, over time, we take for granted. They become just as much a part of us as an arm or a leg.

Bereavement cuts a swathe through these systems and mutilates us just as surely as surgeons mutilate a person when they cut off a limb. To understand the effects of the event we need to know about the individuals involved. It is no good imagining that your bereavement is the same as mine. This is not to say that bereaved people have nothing in common. There are commonalities, and much of this book will help us to identify and examine these. But in the end every bereavement, like every death, is unique and the only person who knows what it is like is the bereaved person. Consequently those who offer help to the bereaved must recognize the limits to their understanding. We must be prepared to let the bereaved explain themselves to us rather than seeing ourselves as the experts who know all the answers.

Fortunately the very act of explaining ourselves to other people is itself therapeutic. While the bereaved are explaining themselves to us, they are also explaining themselves to themselves and this reassessment of life is one of the most important tasks of grieving.

Peter's death did not take place in a social vacuum. He had a wife and children who cared about him and for him. Their presence in the hospice during much of his stay enabled them to support him and he them, but, as often happens, when in the presence of his family Peter was 'putting on a good show' and so were the family. Only when the staff saw them on their own would they talk about their problems.

Similarly, after Peter's death his widow tried to protect her children by keeping her feelings to herself and they too tried to protect her by concealing their own problems. In consequence a family who loved and cared about each other found themselves unable to help each other simply because they cared so much.

In cases such as these, and they are all too common in our society, the help of someone from outside the family, whom they trust, can be invaluable. Often the person will be a doctor, nurse, social worker or other member of the caring team who, because of their involvement with the patient, has earned that trust. Professional carers become key figures and agents of change in the process of transition that the family face. Like the parents of frightened children, we must not back away; we must remain involved and do our best to ensure that the family come through this turning point in their lives as well as possible. If we succeed, we shall have the pleasure of seeing them emerge from the long valley of grief stronger, wiser and more mature than they went into it.

This Book

This book is intended primarily for members of the caring professions and for volunteers who work with the terminally ill[1] and the bereaved. This includes those who work in hospitals and in the community as well as hospice staff and specialist home care teams. Presently many of these people have little training in counselling. The very word is scary. Faced with a person who is dying we feel inadequate: 'What can you say?' The image comes to mind of the 'therapist' who prevents people from going mad, always has a wise word to utter and a magical solution to the slings and arrows of outrageous fortune. How can we emulate such a paragon? Fortunately we do not have to. Counselling is not something done by one person to another. It is more to do with sharing than with solving, with listening rather than uttering, and with fostering growth rather than treating mental illness.

To some degree we are all counsellors. All our lives we have been learning how to cope and to help others cope with problems. Counselling is like parenting in many ways. In other ways it is more

---

1 By 'terminally ill' we mean people who are suffering from a disease that is likely to end fatally and who have now come to the end of any treatment aimed at cure or the prolongation of life. There is no such thing as a 'dying patient' since all people are alive until they happen to be dead, and should be treated as such.

like a profession. The term 'profession' has two distinct meanings: on the one hand it is used to imply an occupation for which one is paid, and on the other a level of commitment, knowledge and skill above that of the amateur. Counsellors may not fall into the first of these categories but they will certainly need to fall into the second if they are to provide skilled and reliable help to a vulnerable group of people.

We hope that this book will do three things: it will help you, the reader, to understand the problems that are likely to arise at times of death and bereavement; it will show you how best to make use of the skills you already have; and it will suggest a range of additional skills which, if you feel comfortable with them, you can use. This last consideration is all important. We are not proposing that the reader must change into a different kind of person. Some people are very good at putting people at their ease by laughing or telling a joke, while another person who attempts the same will only cause embarrassment. It is important that whatever skills you use should be skills with which you genuinely feel comfortable. You should not attempt to become a slavish imitation of another person and should particularly beware of adopting the identity of a psychiatrist or other therapist. None of us should pretend to knowledge that we do not possess and we should be ready to refer on to others those people whose needs we cannot meet.

There is some justification for reserving the term 'Counsellor' (with a capital 'C') for people who have been selected for and passed an approved course of training for the job. Others who provide counselling and use counselling skills, even though they may not have passed an approved course of training, we shall refer to as counsellors (with a small 'c'). To save time we shall refer to the people whom they set out to help as 'clients', although we recognize that many of these will not have sought help for themselves at all (for example, if they are caring for a sick family member). Where appropriate we shall refer to people who happen to be sick as 'patients' because this is the shortest accepted term, but we recognize the danger of alienation which exists in the use of this term. Similarly we shall use the term 'family' to include the family of origin, parents, foster parents, siblings and other close relatives, as well as the family of attachment, the spouses, partners, children and others to whom we are tied by bonds which are usually referred to as 'love' but may not be at all romantic. Together these make up what are commonly and uncomfortably referred to as 'significant others'. We prefer the older designation.

We are aware that many people are first-class counsellors with very little training at all. Others will never become counsellors, perhaps because their own needs are so great that they overwhelm those of their clients. In between there are a great number of people who will benefit from a straightforward account of the commoner problems and of those skills which are useful in counselling the dying and the bereaved. It is for this group that this volume is intended.

Summary

❏   As long as patients are alive their needs will come first, but this does not mean that those of the family should be ignored.

❏   When the patient has died the family must take priority.

❏   Every bereavement, like every death, is unique.

❏   Those who offer help to the bereaved must recognize the limits to their understanding.

❏   The reassessment of one's life is one of the most important tasks of grieving.

❏   Family members often attempt to protect each other by denying their own needs.

❏   By reaching out to the family at turning points in their lives members of the caring team become agents of change.

❏   Counselling is not something done by one person *to* another; it is done *with* another.

❏   Counselling requires a 'professional' level of commitment, knowledge and skill, above that of the amateur.

❏   Counsellors should be ready to refer on to others those whose needs they cannot meet.

1

Families in Transition

It is not only the patient who suffers from serious illness; cancer and other potentially fatal illnesses invade families. The patient's troubles may soon be over; those of the rest of the family may be just beginning. The very attempt to distinguish patients from family members is a distortion, for patients *are* family members, the patient's problems are family problems, and the family's problems are the patient's. I may be dying but my family will live on and be permanently changed by my death.

It follows that the unit of care when someone has a life-threatening illness should be the family (which includes the patient) rather than the patient with other members of the family fitted in if we have the time. This conclusion may seem obvious but it is quite foreign to most people who have been educated in a health care system in which the patient is the focus of care, and it is equally foreign to family members who make a tacit assumption that only the patient matters.

As we saw in the Introduction, when somebody's life is in danger the other members of the family normally rally round in support. They insist on putting the patient first and tend to deny their own needs. Doctors and nurses often do the same, and the result is that we miss an opportunity to help people to prepare themselves for a major transition in their lives. Does that matter? It certainly does and there is a great deal of evidence, from psychiatric practice and research (Parkes, 1996), that major changes in the family, especially if they involve a loss, are turning points that influence the health and adjustment of family members for years and possibly generations to come.

What is a Family?

To understand how these problems come about, it is necessary to look first at what it is that makes a family. A family is very much more than a group of individuals who happen to be related. It is the biological entity which makes us what we are, the social unit from which we arose and take our identity. Whether we like it or not (and many people do not like their families) our families are just as much a part of us as our arms and our legs. Like the amputee, we may learn to do without the other members of our family, and many people in our society are amputated from their families, but this in no way detracts from the fact that the family are an enduring influence in our lives and we in theirs.

The biological function of the family is to act as a support system, a safe social unit, in which children can be born, develop safely into adults and, in their turn, raise another family. Families tend to occupy homes, safe places in which children can be raised and to which they return at times of trouble. Thus the family and the home, between them, are the main source of security for human beings as they are for other social animals.

In the large and complex societies in which most people in the West live today, many children are brought up with only one parent, and those who know both their parents may not see both of them. Many functions of the family have been taken over by the larger society. We turn for our security to the law, the social security office or the health care system at times of trouble and, usually, they can meet our needs and make us safe. Even in the worst of families it is rare for children to die. Consequently, we can take our families for granted. But when things go badly wrong and our secure world is threatened, we find ourselves turning again to the family unit and expecting to find the same care (or lack of care) that we received as children.

Grief is the reaction to loss of a person or thing to whom we are attached. In the next section of this chapter we shall examine how attachments come about and how they are patterned by our experience of life. This will help us to understand the consequences of these attachments coming to an end.

Attachments

Families are held together by attachments, bonds which develop early in life and are maintained throughout life in one form or another. The child's first attachment is usually to its mother and this attachment sets the pattern for all later attachments. By the end of the first year of life every baby has learned a repertoire of behaviour which facilitates attachment. The different components of attachment behaviour, although rooted in instinct, are influenced by experience from the outset. Thus smiling, clinging and following, which maintain proximity to the mother, and crying and searching, which come into operation at times of separation, are affected by the way in which the mother responds. Smiling will be reinforced if it brings about a desired response or extinguished if it is ignored. Mothers who ignore their baby's smiles may still respond to cries. The baby soon learns what works best and becomes a tearful baby or a smiley baby. Within the first two years of life children develop habits of attachment behaviour which influence how they react to the world and how the world, in turn, reacts to them. Once established, the pattern of reaction to separation and loss is difficult to change. In a classic series of experiments the psychologist Mary Ainsworth (1991) has shown that the way in which a child of 18 months reacts when separated for a few minutes from its mother in a strange situation predicts how it will be coping with other relationships 10 years later.

Of course, the mother is not the only important person in the life of a young child. There are some fathers who are better 'mothers' than some mothers and, when women go out to work and others look after the children, the person who does most of the mothering may not be the child's biological mother. But *somebody* should fulfil this role and provide consistent mothering, for only if the carer is consistent in response to the child will the child achieve any sense of life being predictable and of being in control of it.

Mary Ainsworth was a student of John Bowlby, who is rightly regarded as the father of the body of knowledge known as 'attachment theory'. He pointed out that troubles in later life are much more often caused by mothers who foster *insecure attachment* than it is by mothers who reject their children (Bowlby, 1969). Secure attachment occurs when children have learned a reasonable degree of trust both in their mother as a person who will respond to their attachment behaviour, and in themselves as able to survive for a while when the mother is not around. Thus good parents are not just people who protect their children from harm: they also teach them to stand on their own feet in the confident expectation that, in due time, they will tolerate longer and longer periods of separation. Trust in oneself and trust in others both result from patterns of parenting that foster these attitudes.

Insecure attachment occurs when children have learned either that their mother cannot be relied upon to respond to their attachment behaviour or that the world is so dangerous a place that they will always be too weak to cope without her. It is a paradox that, in a world in which most children survive their childhood, so many children grow up with deep feelings of insecurity. This results largely from the fact that mothers themselves feel insecure in their relationships with their children. Perhaps they are too busy or unable to give priority to the child. Some mothers cannot bear their children to cling; they respond to their children's attachment bids by punishing or rejecting them. Such children are forced to inhibit their desire to cry or to hold or cuddle their mother at times of danger and they may appear independent from an early age. In Mary Ainsworth's strange situation test babies take little notice when their mother leaves the room and often ignore her when she returns. But their self-reliance does not protect them from feeling anxious, and their apparent 'independence' is associated with a racing heart and other physical signs of fear. Other babies have mothers who are insensitive to their bids for attention; they show every manifestation of distress when separated from their mother and cling to her in an angry way when she returns. They too are excessively insecure and seem to feel that they have no hope of survival unless they stay close to their mother.

The acid test of attachment is the way a child copes with separation. Securely attached children will tolerate short periods of separation quite well; they may whimper for a short time when their mother leaves the room but, provided she does not stay away too long, they will continue to play with toys, their heart rate will not rise unduly and they will greet her return with a hug and a smile. Securely attached children are more relaxed and adventurous than insecurely attached children; they learn more quickly, do better at school and, in due time, the transition from childhood dependency to adult autonomy proceeds relatively smoothly. By contrast insecurely attached children are generally anxious and insecure; they are often under-achievers, doing less well at school than their intelligence would lead us to expect and, in adolescence, their progress towards a separate existence is painful for all concerned. Both clinging to and angry rejection of parents occur and may alternate in a confusing way. The parents, who have always found this child 'difficult', may make things worse either by punitive rejection or by anxious clinging.

In the world in which humans evolved, children who did not become attached to parents did not survive. This may account for the way in which the patterns of attachment learned in childhood often persist into adult life, as well as for the extraordinary power of the emotions evoked by separation. Having learned to cling to mother in order to survive, the adolescent or young adult may cling to partners and others. Sadly the repertoire of behaviour patterns that worked on mother may not work with other people; clinging may cause the very thing that it was intended to prevent, rejection. Since the clinger has no other means of coping with loss, rejection may then cause him or her to cling all the harder. The consequences may be disastrous to the relationship and evoke feelings of extreme distress in the clinger. In a similar way the person who has learned not to get too close to mother will find it very difficult to tolerate closeness to other people. Having been punished for giving expression to natural urges for a cuddle or a hug, the person will become extremely anxious in sexual or other situations in which proximity is expected. Again the consequences may be disastrous to the relationship and confirm in the 'cold fish' the belief that it is safer not to get close to anybody. In this way attitudes learned in childhood may be reinforced in later life and become self-perpetuating.

It would, however, be wrong to think that people who have been insecurely attached to a parent in childhood are doomed. It is never too late to learn. In childhood the insecurity implanted by one parent is often counteracted by the behaviour of the other, or by siblings and friends. Similarly, in adult life the experience of a good relationship with an understanding lover who, instead of aggravating the problem, behaves in a tolerant and consistent way will provide a kind of 'parenting' which the partner has always lacked. Little by little security is established and the hangovers from childhood fade away.

Attachment and Loss

Threats to life and major losses evoke attachment behaviour at any age and it should not surprise us to find that many of the problems touched upon above will become manifest when somebody is dying. This may create problems but it also provides people with an opportunity to learn better ways of coping with separation and loss. Doctors, nurses and other professionals are no substitute for a good family but we can help the family to 'hold the line' and, when families are acting in dysfunctional ways, we can help them to discover more creative solutions to the problems they face and to break the vicious circles that may have perpetuated the problems.

Whether we like it or not, we are an important source of security to them and will be treated as if we too were part of the family. This will sometimes give us the opportunity to set an example of 'good parenting' that is very different from their experience to date.

Mary Jones was the youngest child of a mother whom she described as an anxious woman who gave the impression that the world was a dreadful and dangerous place. In some ways her mother doted on her, thinking of her as a much-prized but 'delicate' child and 'the baby of the family', but she was also very intolerant of closeness. Mary's main source of security was her father, but even he became anxious about her and overprotective during her teens. In the circumstances it is not surprising that Mary grew up a rather anxious, tidy person and an under-achiever despite her superior intelligence.

When she was 15 years of age, her mother had a 'nervous breakdown'. Mary, feeling very insecure, clung to her first boy-friend, Philip, a bright young man by whom she soon became pregnant. At this time Mary was seen as far too insecure to cope with the responsibility of rearing a young baby and the pregnancy was terminated. Her relationship with Philip continued, however, and, in her later teens she gradually seemed to become more sure of herself. When she was 23, they became engaged.

Then disaster struck. Her father died suddenly and unexpectedly from a myocardial infarction and Mary found herself having to give a great deal of emotional support to her anxious mother. For a while she held herself together, suppressing her own grief and filling her life with activities so as not to think too much about what had happened. Her marriage to Philip took place as planned, three months after her father's death.

It was only then, at a time when everyone was congratulating her and she was supposed to be happy, that she began to get depressed 'for no reason'. She found herself unable to concentrate on her work, her sleep was disturbed by nightmares of spiders and she began to lose weight. As a result she was referred to a Counsellor.

In the event she was seen only twice. At the first interview she spent an hour and a half telling the Counsellor the story of her life. She came across as a very sensible and intelligent young woman who needed to be reassured that the 'depression' from which she was suffering was a very understandable reaction to her father's death and that what she needed, more than anything else, was time to grieve. The Counsellor did not treat her as sick, delicate, weak or in any way inferior. In fact he showed, by his respectful attitude, an appreciation of her achievements and she left feeling stronger rather than weaker.

By the time of the second interview Mary was already a great deal happier. She reported that she had found the first meeting very helpful, she no longer felt a failure and she could understand why she had reacted as she had to her father's death. Her husband, who had accompanied her to the first meeting with the Counsellor, was also less anxious and both they and the Counsellor felt that she would cope well without the need for further help from outside the family.

Mary's case illustrates many of the points we have made. Like all children she soon began to see the world through her mother's eyes, and, since her mother saw her as 'delicate' and detected danger everywhere, it is hardly surprising that Mary did the same. It is hard to concentrate and enjoy school work when you are in a state of anxiety, and Mary's natural intelligence did not bear fruit until she had begun to separate herself from her mother and to learn that she was stronger than she had ever imagined. Her relationship with Philip was mutually respectful and did more than anything else to make her more secure until the vicissitudes of her late teens and her father's death temporarily undermined the progress she had made.

Fear and Grief

Two emotional problems appear in many different forms when people are dying or bereaved: fear and grief. Fear is the normal human reaction to any danger and grief the normal reaction to losses of all kinds, be they of people, parts of the body, or hopes. Both fear and grief need to be recognized and understood if we are to be of any help to the dying and the bereaved. This sounds obvious but a multitude of difficulties arise because people misunderstand these normal emotional states.

Fear

The world in which we evolved was very much more dangerous than the one in which we live today. Predators abounded, food was scarce and we needed to be ready to fight or to run very fast if we were to survive. At any time our hunting, feeding, resting or other habits could be interrupted by danger and we evolved an entire nervous system, the autonomic nervous system, to enable us to switch back and forth between crisis and calm, anxious and vegetative states.

When we apprehend a danger we become restless and hyper-alert; our brain is fully aroused and our attention directed outwards. We take in much more information than is usual and react more quickly. At the same time our autonomic nervous system causes adrenaline and other substances to pour into our blood and sends direct messages to our heart and other organs to ready them for emergency action. As a result, blood is diverted from our intestines into our muscles, which become tense in preparation for violent action, our hearts beat faster and more strongly, and our skin flushes and sweats to counteract the build up of heat that will accompany vigorous activity. The flow of saliva in the mouth diminishes, as do most other digestive functions. In effect we become a highly sensitive fighting or fleeing machine.

These reactions have enabled humankind to survive but they are of less use to us today. We can seldom deal with the dangers of modern life by fighting or fleeing. In fact the physical features of anxiety and fear create fresh problems for us and are often mistaken for 'symptoms'. We are 'jumpy' and 'fidgety', unable to concentrate, relax or sleep, and if we do get to sleep we remain restless throughout the night. Our heart palpitates, we sweat and flush, our tense muscles soon start to ache or tremble and the dryness in our mouths makes it difficult to talk clearly. Because our body and mind are attuned to danger we easily misperceive danger where none exists. In other words, a set of responses which show that our minds and bodies are responding normally become seen as symptoms of abnormality. They then become another source of fear, so that the reaction tends to perpetuate and aggravate itself.

It is worth making a distinction between fear and anxiety, although the two do tend to go together. Fear has an object: we are frightened *of* something. Anxiety does not have a particular object: it is a general state in which many things may seem dangerous. Because one danger often leads to another, fear often triggers anxiety, and because anxious people are on the alert for danger, anxiety can trigger fear.

The decision to fight or to flee arises out of our analysis of the dangerous situation. If we have a chance of winning we can afford to get aggressive; if not, we had better submit or run away. It follows that fear and anger often go together, as do fear and depression (the emotional reaction to helplessness).

Fear, by causing us to focus our attention on a possible danger, does help us to prepare ourselves for that danger. This has been termed 'the work of worrying'. For instance, people who have anxiously examined the likely consequences of major surgery are better prepared for the postoperative period than people who have not undertaken this painful task. It follows that members of health care teams should not over-protect people by concealing from them information that will worry them.

Grief

Grief, like fear, has an object, the lost person. As we have seen above, whenever we are separated for any length of time from people to whom we are attached, we suffer an emotion of pining or 'separation fear'. This takes priority over most other thoughts and behaviour. We stop all other activities in order to cry aloud and to search for the one who is lost and, in most circumstances, this will improve our chances of finding them. Only in the relatively rare event that they are permanently lost does this activity become redundant.

There then follows a long series of emotional struggles which Worden (1982) terms the 'tasks of grieving'. The intelligent human adult knows very well that it is pointless to cry aloud and to search for a dead person, but this does not prevent us from experiencing a powerful urge to do just that. Our heart and our head are in conflict and the outcome is a compromise: the cry becomes stifled to a sob, and the search becomes a restless tendency to go over the events leading up to the loss as if, even now, we could find out what has gone wrong and put it right. We treasure reminders of our loss and visit places which we associate with the dead person as if we could find them again. At times we may think we see or hear them but these misperceptions soon lead to disappointment and another 'pang' of grief.

The search for the lost person may continue in dreams in which the dead person may seem vividly alive, but this too will be followed by an unhappy awakening. In states of drowsiness it is common for people to hallucinate the dead person but, unlike the hallucinations of mental illness, these 'hypnagogic hallucinations' disappear when the bereaved person becomes fully awake. On the other hand the sense of the presence of the dead person somewhere nearby, which is also very common, can persist.

In the early stages of bereavement,[1] people are intellectually aware that the person they love is dead but they say, 'It doesn't seem real'. They will simultaneously know and not know; 'I know she's gone but I can't accept it,' said one man whose wife had died. This split between knowing and accepting seems to indicate that it takes time to make real inside the self an event that is already an established reality outside the self.

Freud coined the term 'grief work' for the process by which people gradually close this gap and one is tempted to think that this must be the same thing as 'worry work'. Certainly there is evidence from many sources that people who allow themselves to weep and to express grief will come through the grieving process more quickly than those who avoid grieving by keeping busy or by other means.

Worden (1982) describes 'accepting the reality of loss' and 'working through the pain of grief' as the first two tasks of grieving and it is useful to bear them in mind when counselling the bereaved. They are, however, two aspects of one and the same process and should not be seen as distinct from each other.

Nobody can grieve all the time. From the earliest stages bereaved people must eat, sleep and undertake a host of responsibilities and actions that compete with grieving and may enable them to have some respite from grief. At times all bereaved people need to put their grief aside for a while. It is only if the avoidance of grieving is persistent that problems are likely to arise.

Just as fear is often accompanied by anger or depression, so too is grief. It may seem strange that people can treat bereavement as a

1   The idea that grief follows a series of stages arose from Bowlby and Robertson's observations of young children separated from their mothers. Bowlby and Parkes subsequently applied the same model to bereavement in adult life and the idea was then picked up by Elizabeth Kübler-Ross, who described her well known 'stages of dying'. The idea helped to make it clear that grief is not a state but a process through which people pass. Unfortunately it also gave the impression of an inexorable progression through which all bereaved people or terminally ill people *have* to pass if they are to come to terms their loss. In actual fact people move back and forth between the phases of grief and there is great variation from one person to another. We have not found the concept of 'phases' or 'stages' particularly helpful in counselling and they are not, therefore, detailed here. For a more comprehensive account of these and other theories about bereavement the reader is referred to Parkes (1996).

battle to be won but some do this. They may seize on something which a doctor or nurse did to the dying patient and become extremely angry, as if they could undo the harm that has been done. Some may blame themselves for the death, as if, by punishing themselves, they could make everything come right again. Depression, by contrast, often becomes more pronounced at a later stage in the course of grieving. As the griever begins to accept the full reality and irreversibility of the loss, fear gives place increasingly to depression. At this time the bereaved are more fully aware than they have been of the extent of their loss but they have not yet begun to fill the gap left by the person who is gone from their lives.

Internal Change

To understand the nature of that gap we need to look again at the ways in which the people we love become part of us. Each one of us, from the day we are born, are building inside ourselves a model of the world. Before long we can identify tables and chairs and windows and achieve a degree of control over the world around us by comparing incoming sensations with our internal memory of these things, recognizing what is happening and behaving accordingly. Our sense of life having meaning derives from the many ways in which our internal world, and the plans that soon become a part of that internal world, fit the world around us.

Of course, our internal worlds contain a great deal more than tables and chairs and windows. They include everything that we assume to be true about the world, everything we take for granted. This includes habits of thought about people as well as things and it also includes our view of ourselves.

The world around us is constantly changing but most of the changes are relatively minor. In fact one of the pleasures of life is to add to our internal model of the world by visiting new places and doing new things. Only when we are faced with a massive loss, as when we lose a limb, go blind or learn that our spouse is dead, are we likely to have to undertake a radical revision of our internal model of the world, and this is a painful and time-consuming business. For a long time after the loss the amputee has to be very careful not to tread on a leg that is not there, blind people repeatedly find themselves turning towards a sound, expecting to see what has made it, the widow lays the table for two, then realizes that there are not two people to eat breakfast. Each time this happens people are brought up short, painfully aware that they can no longer rely on their internal models to furnish them with an accurate picture of the world. More poignantly they become aware of the extent to which the meaning of many activities which can be continued depended on some basic assumption that no longer holds true. The house-proud housewife loses interest in her house when there is no longer someone at home to appreciate it. The cancer patient may see no point in getting out of bed unless there is a reasonable chance of getting better.

Samuel Johnson (quoting Richard Hooker) once said, 'Change is not made without inconvenience, even from worse to better' (Boswell, 1791). Our internal model of the world is our only means of comprehending, relating to and controlling the world; when we can no longer rely on it we feel mutilated and lost. Life itself seems to have lost its meaning; the world is 'upside down', and the familiar world seems strangely unfamiliar.

Then, slowly and intermittently, we begin to rebuild our world; appetites and interests return, we discover new and formerly unused talents and we realize that we are stronger than we had thought. Most important of all, we learn that we have not lost everything that came with the person who is gone. When the bereaved say that someone 'lives on in my memory,' they are referring to something very real. The people we love remain a constant source of inspiration. Just as the developing child can eventually separate from the mother because he or she has learned to be like her, so a widow can think, 'What would my husband say about this?' or 'It's almost as if I had him inside my head telling me what to do.'

It is these changes which Worden describes as the tasks of 'adjusting to an environment in which the deceased is missing' and 'emotionally relocating the deceased'. Again it is useful to bear these tasks in mind when counselling the bereaved but we should not see them as two distinct activities; they are two sides of the same coin.

Loss of Meaning

Most people, when they speak of their life as having a meaning, are speaking of that sense of being 'on course' that most of us have most of the time. Some will phrase this in religious language; they will see themselves as being at peace with God and of having a feeling of relating to or being looked after by God. Others have no such faith; their sense of meaning derives more from the basic assumptions which underlie and make sense of the more super-ficial assumptions. These include satisfactions that come from fulfilling roles as parent, friend, worker, spouse or other types of social relationship. Scratch a little deeper and we find that these roles, which all involve other people, have some purpose or value which transcends the gains of immediate gratification. In other words, they imply a frame of reference that extends beyond the self and involves commitment to some greater whole. It is this, we suggest, that distinguishes the spiritual from the psychological.

Threats to life and bereavements can undermine both the religious and the more secular type of faith. The religious may find themselves at odds with God, questioning the justice of God's care and doubting God's existence or goodness. Those without such faith may still find that the meanings which they had taken for granted are shattered. Not only do they doubt their ability to function in their accustomed roles, they may even question the value of the roles. The man who has worked hard to save money for his retirement may find that both retirement and work are meaningless once the wife who was to have shared it with him has gone.

It is hardly surprising that death and bereavement commonly give rise to a collapse of what Marris (1982) calls 'the structure of meaning'. Some of these meanings are, of course, trivial or unworthy. Maybe we were wrong to think of God as a kind of guardian angel who would keep us safe as long as we said our prayers regularly and went to church. Maybe we should not have imagined that disasters only happen to bad people. In this sense the feeling as if a house of cards has collapsed is quite justified. If it was truly a house of cards perhaps it should collapse: only then can we be rebuild our structure of meaning on a firmer footing. And this, we hope, is what can happen. It is for this reason that 'suffering is good for the soul' and people emerge from the disasters of life in a sadder but wiser frame of mind. But there are no guarantees. Some will remain embittered and withdrawn, unable to cope with the chaos of a ruined world; others will cling in childish ways to their old assumptions and ignore the evidence of reality.

Our role as counsellors may be to facilitate the spiritual struggle by trying to provide people with a safe place or relationship in which to carry it out.

Whereas the newly bereaved feel weak, helpless and crippled by grief, the veteran who has come through bereavement often emerges stronger, wiser and more mature than before. But the transition is never easy and can lead to disaster as well as growth. Grief is not an illness from which we recover. We are all permanently changed by grief. In one sense it never ends; even years after a bereavement, finding a picture in a drawer or meeting an old friend in the street can bring on another pang of grief. Having said that, there is no doubt that something changes. As one bereaved person said, 'It doesn't go away, but you learn to live with it.'

Summary

❏ The unit of care when someone has a life-threatening illness should be the family (which includes the patient) rather than the patient with other members of the family fitted in if we have the time.

❏ When things go badly wrong and our secure world is threatened, we find ourselves turning again to the family unit and expecting to find the same care (or lack of care) that we received when we grew up as children.

❏ The child's first attachment to its mother sets the pattern for all later attachments.

❏ The achievement of secure attachments later in life can undo much of the damage done by earlier insecurity.

❏ Threats to life and bereavement undermine security and can be expected to evoke the characteristic patterns of attachment to which each person is liable.

❏ In the environment in which humankind evolved the bodily reaction to danger improved our chances of survival. In the modern world fear and its accompaniments are often seen as dysfunctional and likely to be interpreted as symptoms requiring treatment. This can increase the fear.

❏ Anxiety, or the work of worrying, helps us to prepare for danger and change.

❏ Health care teams should not over-protect people by concealing from them information that may worry them.

❏ The need to express grief may conflict with the need to control or avoid grieving.

❏ People who express grief often come through the process of grieving more quickly than those who avoid or repress it. Hence two of Worden's tasks of mourning are accepting the fact of loss and working through the pain of grief.

❏ Hypnagogic hallucinations of the lost person and vivid dreams of them are common and do not denote pathology.

❏ Major losses face people with the need to change a great number of habits of thought and assumptions about the world. This takes time and energy and gives rise to Worden's other two tasks of mourning, adjusting to an environment in which the deceased is missing and emotionally relocating the deceased.

❏ Because a sense of meaning or purpose derives from a sense of fit between the world that is and these assumptions, major losses easily undermine it.

❏ Through revising and rebuilding our assumptive world we discover new structures of meaning.

❏ We are all permanently change by grief; some may be crippled but many emerge stronger and wiser.

2

The Caring Team

As we have seen, the family exists to care for its members and our families are usually the first people to whom we turn at times of trouble. The main body of care given to people with terminal illness is provided by their families within the family home. Doctors, nurses and other professional carers remain the second line of care. Even so, help from outside the family is always needed, either because of the expert knowledge that is required to meet the complex needs of a family facing terminal illness or because the family is absent or unable to fulfil its traditional functions. It follows that the professional team must be prepared not only to provide expertise but also to assess the need for support and to see that it is provided, either by ourselves or by some other appropriate person.

In much of this book we shall be discussing how to assess the need for support, how to provide it and how to organize it. Here we look at the team of professional carers as a psychological unit in its own right, how it functions and how its own needs can be met. No matter how effective we are at meeting the needs of other people, a team that does not also meet the needs of its own members will soon fall apart.

Medical and nursing teams, like families, have their own structure, hierarchy, culture, rituals, systems of belief and history. Much of the time these succeed in enabling the teams to meet the needs of patients and team members, but there are also times when they fail to meet these needs and those of the patient's family. This often occurs because the philosophy of the team was developed for a different set of problems and circumstances.

Three Philosophies of Care

The system of medical and nursing care with which most of us are familiar developed in order to combat disease and repair damage.

Most people who go to a doctor want to be cured of an affliction. They may not be seeking emotional support or personal growth. They may delay seeking help because they fear that the cure may itself be painful, time consuming and expensive, but, in the end, they are prepared to put up with these things for the sake of a return to health. When they go to a professional there is an implicit contract that this is what we shall provide.

The providers of health care know that not all illnesses are curable and that, despite all the advances of modern science, 100% of people will eventually die. What is more, before they die they will often suffer lasting disablement. We feel distinctly uncomfortable when we know that we are not going to be able to fulfil our part of the contract, and find it difficult to be open about such matters. To tell someone that they are incurable or that they will probably die of the disease for which they are consulting us is painful for us as well as for our clients. Yet if we do not do this we become a kind of confidence trickster, a 'quack' who offers what he cannot deliver. We may even be tempted to give treatments or carry out operations that will do more harm than good, simply to maintain the pretence and satisfy the patient's wish for magic.

The situation is a little easier if, despite our inability to cure, we have something else to offer. Systems of care which are not aimed at cure need to be very different to those that are. We need to be clear in our own minds what it is that we can offer and, in most instances, we should make this clear to our clients. They have a right to know what kind of a package they are buying.

Apart from cure-orientated care there are two other packages that we can reasonably offer. On the one hand there are services which aim to help people to live with their disabilities, restoring function where possible, or helping them to organize their lives around a new set of assumptions about the world; these are the rehabilitation services. On the other, there are services that recognize that it is fruitless to invest a great deal of time and energy in restoring function; the focus must be on relieving distress and helping patient and family to come to terms with the ending of the patient's life. It is this last alternative that is the basis of palliative care, which, in our view, involves very much more than palliation.[1]

1 Palliative care has been defined as: 'The active total care of patients whose disease is not responsive to curative treatment. Control of pain and other symptoms, and of psychological, social and spiritual problems is paramount. The goal of palliative care is achievement of the best quality of life for patients and their families' (World Health Organization, 1990).

Of course, we will not always know what is best. It may take some time for the prognosis to become clear and both we and the patient may have to live with uncertainty. At such times we tend to take the most optimistic view and adopt a philosophy of care that may later have to change. We do nobody a favour, however, if we persist in courses of treatment when we know that they are eventually going to lead to disappointment.

Table 2.1 compares these three philosophies of care. We call them philosophies because they are very much more than techniques. They embody the way we, the patient and the family view ourselves and our work, the rewards we obtain and the way we are viewed by others. Thus *cure-orientated care* is focused on the patient and is relatively brief. Because no long-term adjustment is likely to be necessary in patients' lives there is no need for them to undertake a major revision of their view of the world or to grieve. Their existing faith in the meaning of their life may be shaken and they may welcome spiritual help in the short term but ultimate meanings are unlikely to change. It is appropriate for staff and family to provide reassurance and support, to encourage the patient to keep a 'stiff upper lip' through the trials of the illness but to understand and continue support if they are unable to do this. The family need to relieve the patient of major obligations only temporarily and their lives are unlikely to be affected in the long term. The staff may need to make use of all the technical skills they possess in order to save life and ensure recovery. At such time strong leadership is needed from above and the leaders may bear heavy responsibility if things go wrong: the patient's life is literally in their hands. Unless things go wrong the emotional demands made upon the staff are not great.

Care aimed at *rehabilitation* is very different. Here the main focus is initially on getting patient and family through the impact of the illness and its treatments and then helping them to adjust to the major changes in their lives that follow. The main burden usually falls on the patient but the family will often have to undertake major changes in their lives and should be involved from the start. The aim is to ensure that the patient becomes as autonomous as possible given the circumstances and it is vital to minimize dependence on the team and on family members. Patients need help to express grief for what they are losing before they begin the slow process of rebuilding their internal assumptions about the world. This may entail a painful spiritual struggle as people come to realize that they can no longer take things for granted.

Table 2.1. *Philosophies of care*

	Cure	Rehabilitation	Palliation
Object	Cure	Restore maximum functioning	Relieve distress and support transition
Focus	Patient	Patient and family	Family, which includes patient
Duration	Transient	Until autonomy of patient is attained (may be lifelong)	Until family grief is resolved
Patient's response	'Stiff upper lip'	Express grief then work at rebuilding	Express grief then accept and let go
Spiritual impact	May be shaken	Loss of meaning transiently but time to rebuild	Loss of meaning and patient has little time to rebuild
Spiritual help	Patient may need short-term help	Long-term help needed by patient and family	Patient needs urgent help, family long-term help
Family, short term	Support patient	Support patient take over roles	'Stiff upper lip' and hold fort
Family, long term	None needed	Relinquish support and encourage autonomy	Express grief then work at rebuilding
Team skills	Technical	Inter-personal	Inter-personal
Team leadership	Hierarchical	Patient-led	Power shared with family

In the long term it is important to encourage patients to take responsibility for their lives and they should therefore be treated as the team leader whenever possible. This requires a major change in attitude on the part of staff who normally like to think that it is we who are in charge. We need to use all the interpersonal skills at our command if we are to achieve satisfactory results. The implications of this model of care have been well described in Miller and Gwynne's study of institutions for the chronic sick, *A Life Apart* (1972). The philosophy works well for those who are capable of achieving a reasonable degree of autonomy but tends to break down when applied to people who are on a course towards death and whose bodily functions are failing. They easily come to see themselves and to be seen by others as failures.

Palliative care, which is the main topic of this book, contains two elements: palliation (relief of suffering), and support in transition (the psychological and spiritual change that takes place in a family whenever one of its members is dying or dead). The first requires expert, sensitive and continued appraisal of all the sources of physical and mental suffering that exist in patients and families, with the object of relieving this suffering. The second implies an equally sensitive appraisal of the psychological and spiritual needs of the family (which includes the patient), with the object of supporting any who may need our help. Thus we are both therapists and agents of change.

Involvement with the family is essential, as their needs may be very great. The major challenge to the meaning of life which faces both patients and family members means that they often need spiritual help although they may not always seek it. This implies that staff need to have thought through their own attitude to spiritual issues and to be open to discuss these. It does *not* mean that they have to have a blinkered or narrow religious faith which is intolerant of the beliefs of others.

It may be difficult to ascertain who is ultimately responsible for care. Sometimes it is important for staff to be in charge, in order to reduce anxiety in patients and family members, but we should be ready to relinquish this control as soon as it is no longer needed. At other times it will be patients who must be given the opportunity to take charge of their own lives and to 'look after' the family. If, however, the patient is too sick or tired to take a lead it may be more appropriate to encourage a family member to accept responsibility. Again, our tendency to see ourselves as in charge is dangerous and we need to learn an appropriately respectful attitude towards the others involved. The essential philosophy is one of sharing power, involving ourselves in the lives of people who are often in great distress and hanging in with them through a major turning point in their lives. This can be emotionally demanding on staff and requires a well integrated system of support for staff as well as for patients and families. An example of such a system will be described later in this chapter.

Patients with potentially fatal illness such as cancer and AIDS may require any of these three philosophies of care at different times and, while it is often possible to move people from one dedicated unit to another in order to provide the optimum care, this is not always the case and staff in any unit need to be capable of providing the type of care that is needed, regardless of the setting. For this reason it is desirable for staff to become familiar with all three types of care and to be clear in their own minds which philosophy they are adopting at a particular time.

Unless staff can make the mental adjustments that are necessary whenever we switch from cure orientation to a rehabilitation orientation or palliative care orientation we will repeatedly find ourselves acting in ways that are anti-therapeutic and personally undermining. These mental adjustments are not easy for staff or patients. The mother of a baby who dies on a maternity ward is a grim reminder to staff and fellow patients that not every mother will leave the ward with a new baby. She, as well as the staff, feel that they have let the side down. Similarly a patient on a surgical ward who is dying from a terminal cancer may be ignored by fellow patients and avoided by staff who feel that they have nothing to offer.

For this reason alone it is highly desirable for staff who work in such settings to receive proper training and, ideally, to spend time working in hospices or other settings in which they have the opportunity to learn by experience the implications of different philosophies of care. It is often difficult for staff to give the kind of care which they may observe in a hospice. The dominant philosophy of care on their ward may be cure or rehabilitation orientated. Lack of privacy and pressure of work may all make it seem like a Herculean task to offer people the time, privacy and peace which they need if they are to change course. Even so, there may be much that can be done and we should not allow our desire for the best to drive out the possible. If we are clear in our own minds what is needed, we may find a variety of ways of improving care, perhaps by creating a peaceful corner of the ward

that is kept free of machines and instruments, where patients who
are close to death are treated with as much respect as possible and
where relatives can feel that they are not getting in the way of busy
staff.

Finding the Right Distance

Our willingness to become involved in family issues does not mean
that we *have* to. There are many patients and family members who
are quite able to cope without our help and others who will not
accept it even if they need it. We have no right to force ourselves on
others or to intrude uninvited into their families. We do, however,
have a responsibility to reach out to the family, to find out who they
are, to assess their needs and to make clear to them our willingness
to become involved and to support them through this turning
point in their lives.

In every human interaction there is a 'right distance'. Move in too
close and the other person will feel intruded upon; back away too
far and they will feel alienated or rejected. The 'right distance'
varies with the nature of the relationship and the circumstances,
and it is constantly changing so that a distance that feels right at
one time may be uncomfortable at another. Thus, people who are
nervous or afraid will usually want to be close to people they trust
and distant from those they distrust. As their confidence increases
they may let go of the trusted ones and permit a closer contact with
strangers or other potentially dangerous persons. This is very
obvious when people are sick. Some will cling to their doctors and
nurses, whom they regard as a main source of security; others, who
may see us as sources of physical or mental pain, will keep their
distance.

Problems arise when the distance feels 'right' for one person and
'wrong' for the other. Thus staff who see it as part of their role to
get close to patients need to be careful not to force themselves on
people whose trust they have not yet earned. Conversely staff who
are tired or themselves strung up and near the end of their tether
may find it very hard to satisfy the need for closeness of a sick
person or frightened relative.

It is important to distinguish wants from needs. A person will
sometimes want something that is bad for them and there are times
when it is not disrespectful to point this out. 'I want to help you
but I need a breathing space' or 'You want me to stay close but you

are actually quite safe without me' are both possible ways of responding but they are easily misinterpreted and great sensitivity and tact are needed in clarifying and managing appropriate distancing.

Inevitably compromise and delays will occur from time to time and there is seldom harm in this provided the needs of both parties are met in the long run. If, however, it is clear that a caregiver is not going to be able to meet the needs for closeness of a client, then he or she must always seek someone who can. Similarly we should not hesitate to seek help for ourselves if we feel that our needs cannot be met.

The Needs of the Team

As we saw in the last chapter, the function of the family is to be a support to its members at times of trouble and, when we offer ourselves in this role, we are offering to become an extension of the family. This may be difficult in a world in which doctors and nurses who get attached to their patients are seen as 'unprofessional' and in which even attachments to fellow professionals are frowned upon.

For this reason it is important to look closely at the nature of the relationships that arise in palliative care and to consider what dangers and rewards these bring about. It is important for all professional carers to be clear in their own minds what type of commitment is wise, safe and kind, and what unwise, unsafe and unkind.

Relationships within the team are as important to us as relationships with patients and their families. They too involve mutual commitment and appropriate distance/closeness. In this instance it is even more difficult to recognize discrepancies between wants and needs and to communicate them to each other. A senior nurse who says to a junior, 'You may want to stay late in order to look after Mrs X but you need to get off duty' may be seen as interfering with care and disrespecting her colleague's right to choose how she uses her time. Yet if she does not do this she may fail to protect her junior from the effects of over-commitment. It is the duty of senior staff to monitor the extent to which junior staff may be sacrificing their own needs to those of their patients. It is even more difficult for junior staff to support seniors by warning them when they suspect a similar failure to recognize their own needs.

The care of dying and bereaved people is a great challenge. It can be the most stressful part of our work, but it can also be the most rewarding. The rewards are likely to outweigh the stress only if our needs for support are met. If we do not have sufficient support our work will be affected and we will find it increasingly difficult to fulfil our objectives.

Problems arise when:

- situations and events in our personal lives affect our ability to cope and particularly to listen to or get close to others;
- we meet situations that cause us to revisit aspects of our own experience of loss;
- pressure of work causes divided loyalties between the needs of patients and the demands of the institution;
- we feel that the caring, listening part of the work is less valued by others than 'doing';
- team management is ineffective.

Support is essential to enable team members to deal with difficulties and minimize stress. If we do not receive feedback, positive as well as critical, it is hard to feel valued and to know whether we are fulfilling our role. It is important to feel that effective communication and the use of counselling skills are valued by the team and by the institution in which we work. Working with terminally ill people and their families causes much anxiety. It is always difficult to judge whether we are communicating/counselling well enough and this becomes much harder if our colleagues seem to value this less than the 'doing' part of the work. Without support it is unlikely that we will develop confidence in our abilities.

It is often assumed that caring for the dying and the bereaved must be depressing and stressful to staff and while, from time to time, this may be so, most people who work in hospices and palliative care teams find them rather less stressful than other branches of medicine and nursing. The reason is clear: the supportive, caring environment that does so much to alleviate the fears of patients and family members also provides a supportive environment for the staff. When problems arise for us, as they will in the best of families, they are just as likely to result from the frustrations and griefs arising from day-to-day interactions with fellow staff members as they are to result from the frustrations and griefs arising out of our care of patients and their families.

Grief and Burn-out in Staff

It is worth making a distinction between the problem of grief and the problem of burn-out, for the two are often confused. Grief, as we have seen, is the normal reaction to losses of all kinds. Following all but the most trivial of losses it is necessary to grieve if we are not to store up problems for ourselves, and this usually means that we must talk about the loss and share the feelings that then arise. There are some people who can grieve in private and others who can express their feelings indirectly, by laughter or vigorous physical activity, but the feelings must be expressed somehow. This is a human need and applies no matter what professional training we may have received.

Unfortunately the very things that make us proud to be a caregiver, such as the image of selfless love or of heroic battle against the dangers of pain and death, make it difficult for us to express emotions which we see as 'selfish' or 'babyish'. Consequently we behave as if we had no need to feel or express the sadness, anger, guilt and fear which are normal reactions to the losses we face. We do this by:

• being macho, denying negative feelings and maintaining a rigid control,
• avoiding attachments that may cause grief, keeping our distance and restricting our role to that of a technician, and
• keeping our feelings to ourselves.

To a certain degree these defences do work. They enable us to get through dire emergencies without 'breaking down' and they help us to believe that we are the supermen and superwomen that we, and our patients, would like us to be. We may even attempt to inflict our ways of coping on other caregivers, criticizing them if they behave differently and feeling very threatened if they suggest that other alternatives are possible.

A psychologist was consulted by a newly appointed senior nurse about a member of her team who had been seen crying with a patient. 'I am worried about Alice,' she said, 'I don't think she is suited to this kind of nursing'. The psychologist, who knew the nurse well, attempted to reassure her. She pointed out that Alice had been able to stay with the patient and give support, despite her tears, and that this may have been an appropriate way to

*behave in the circumstances. Alice had not seen anything wrong
with her tears and neither, apparently, had the patient. Un-
convinced by this reply the senior nurse repeated her opinion to
the medical director and was surprised to find that she too saw
nothing wrong with Alice's reaction.*

*Some weeks later the senior nurse's own mother died in a
nearby hospital. She subsequently remarked to the psychologist,
'You know, you were quite right. When my mother died one of the
ward staff was in tears and I suddenly realized that she really
cared. That did more to restore my faith in nursing than anything
that has happened to me for a long time.' This experience helped
her to develop greater sensitivity in her own work and to become
a very supportive member of staff.*

In reality the kind of grief which members of the caring professions
experience in their daily life seldom prevents them from continuing
to function. Occasionally grief may touch us more deeply and some
time off may be needed, but usually only for a short time. Those
responsible for managing the team need to know when to support
those staff who need space and time to grieve. If individual
capabilities are respected the team will grow in strength and
maturity. If, on the other hand, team managers react in a rejecting,
angry way towards staff who show their feelings, they will undermine the morale of the team and increase the risk of 'burn out'.

Burn-out

Burn-out is not a psychiatric illness but it can increase the risk of
psychological problems. It can affect individuals or entire teams. It
is responsible for much of the high rate of drop-out among nurses
in training and may even contribute to the incidence of alcoholism,
drug abuse and suicide among doctors. It should, therefore, be
taken very seriously.

Table 2.2 compares the features of burn-out with those of normal
grief. Burn-out is a chronic state rather than an acute one, and it is
easily missed because its symptoms are hidden. It is usually
manifested as low-grade depression, irritability and withdrawal.
Sufferers may become bitter and liable to frequent episodes of
anger or they may simply lose their enthusiasm and become tired
and listless. Their concentration and judgement are impaired and
they often find ways to avoid their responsibilities. Staff members
who were previously 'on the ball' and active members of the team

Table 2.2. *Grief and burn-out compared*

Grief	Burn-out
Acute	Chronic
Hope retained	Hope lost
Help accepted	Help refused
Promotes closeness	Promotes distancing
Improves team cohesion	Undermines team
Fosters understanding	Evokes alienation
Ultimate gain in maturity	Ultimate loss of self-esteem

may seem to have lost their 'spark' and may fail to back up their colleagues. They lose their confidence in themselves and their trust in others.

Burn-out is insidiously infectious, particularly if it affects senior members of staff. Junior staff quickly become bitter and critical of seniors who do not support them. This may undermine their authority, cause rifts within the team and aggravate a bad situation. The entire team may be unable to care effectively for its patients and merely conduct physical and routine aspects of care without commitment or concern. Once established, group burn-out tends to aggravate and perpetuate itself. Such situations account for many of the examples of cruelty and neglect which bring discredit on the 'caring' professions. More often they lead to resignations and collapse of morale.

Burn-out can be caused by any situation which lastingly deprives staff of hope or reasonable reward. People will tolerate frustration, grief and stress as long as they know that it will be relieved and that their efforts are appreciated. We may even grow closer together and learn to work well as a team *because* of the stress, but only so long as we see a purpose in doing so. We can accept failure in our attempts to relieve misery and pain from time to time provided the successes outweigh the failures.

The balance will change if people become so overloaded with work that they cannot do the very things that make their work worthwhile for themselves and the people for whom they care. Often pressure makes it difficult to communicate with and support patients and their families. When wards are intolerably busy over a prolonged period senior staff must demand that respite is given to allow staff time to recover their strength and resilience. When there is pressure from managers to keep the beds filled so that there is no time to say a mental 'goodbye', or when staff who spend time talking to patients are blamed for wasting time and the whole team are having to cut corners, the risk of burn-out will increase. Staff who find themselves scapegoating unpopular patients, avoiding interaction with patients and families who need them and getting irritable with each other are on a course towards burn-out and help is urgently needed. Part of the success of hospices in maintaining high morale stems from the insistence of senior staff on limiting the number of beds in use when occupancy levels have been high for a long period. It is time that staff in hospitals took a similar stand.

The first person to whom staff turn for help is likely to be their supervisor. Supervision helps staff see what is happening. Is the problem with the staff member, with the system, or both? What effect is the overload having upon their personal lives and upon the quality of care that they can give to the patients with whom they are already involved? If the problem is primarily with the staff member, a skilled supervisor can help to look behind the complaint of overload to the hidden drives and motivation of the professional. Is the pursuit of perfection preventing him or her from achieving a reasonable satisfaction with the work? An awareness of what it is reasonable to expect of oneself can help prevent burn-out. Staff are then able to find the confidence to balance their work and private lives without feeling guilt because they cannot personally meet all the demands made upon them.

At times, staff members may suffer personal loss or find themselves under some other stress which may have nothing to do with their work environment but may, even so, make it hard for them to continue to give the care that is needed and expected of them. They too may be vulnerable to burn-out. It is most important for supervisors and other senior staff to be sensitively aware of this possibility and to ensure that anyone who is in this situation is given time off and the opportunity to talk their problems through with someone they trust.

Support must be given to help staff to deal with the griefs that are a normal part of their work. It needs to be multidimensional and no one strategy will suit all members. Diversity ensures that people will feel safe enough to use and develop their skills and recognize when they need to seek additional help. In the following section a number of ways of providing a supportive environment are described. Together, they provide a framework for developing sound and safe practice.

Informal Support

On an everyday basis we need to treat each other with the same respect that we give to patients and clients. In a healthy team people will have time for each other amid the busy atmosphere. Report sessions should allow space to talk about feelings as well as actions but this will only be possible in a non-judgemental atmosphere.

Managers can do much to foster an informal, supportive environment. Arrivals and departures of staff cause insecurity within the team and new members need to feel welcomed and appreciated. Like births and deaths, arrivals and departures should be marked with rituals to help new members to join the team and to help the team to separate from and say 'goodbye' to those who are leaving. These rituals, along with celebrations to mark important personal or team events, help to consolidate the team and make the members feel cared about, and cared for. Support must also be provided in structured and more formal ways.

Formal Support

There are many ways of integrating the provision of support into our work.

Appraisal

Formal appraisal, usually annual, provides the opportunity for staff to reflect upon the work with their managers. Usually both staff member and line manager complete an appraisal form and use it for the basis of the discussion. This allows the staff to comment on the way they feel they are fulfilling their role, their personal development over the year, their training needs and to outline their goals for the coming year. It gives both parties a legitimate opportunity to give and receive feedback and minimizes un-channelled complaining. The person initiating the appraisal should be mindful that staff dread criticism. This stems from those early experiences of parental judgement, or waiting outside the head-teacher's study. It follows that feedback will be more effective if it starts with positive affirmation before proceeding to areas where knowledge and skills may need to be developed. If we never receive feedback, it is difficult to assess whether we are meeting expectations or to identify further training needs.

Peer support groups

Peer support groups usually meet weekly or fortnightly. It is important that the group should feel safe. It can be difficult to meet the needs of all the members of a multidisciplinary team in one group. Junior staff may find it difficult to speak openly in front of their seniors and vice versa, so we recommend having more than one group available to staff. Group members are usually quick to agree not to discuss matters arising in the group with non-members, but in practice the issue of confidentiality can prove more difficult than it sounds. Should members discuss what has happened in the group with other members? One ward sister revealed deep personal sadness at the death of a patient. She was highly embarrassed to be stopped in the corridor by another member of the group on the following day and to be hugged and asked whether she was feeling any better. Other nurses heard and observed the interchange and became concerned. In this example, the ward sister felt that she had not been allowed to contain her feelings within the group and that confidentiality had in effect been broken.

The agenda for discussion should be set by the group members. The emphasis should be on exploring the impact of the work, and members should be encouraged to express their thoughts and feelings about their work. It is not a therapeutic group and the personal problems of members are relevant only if they are affecting their work. Even then it may be preferable to deal with such problems outside the group once they have been identified. The group facilitator should be trained in group work and will usually be seen as less threatening if he or she has no management responsibility and comes from outside the organization.

It is worth considering the following factors before deciding to set up a group:

- Should staff attend in their own time or work time? In our view staff support is so important that it should be a recognized part of our employment. It is, of course, essential that other responsibilities are covered effectively during groups or members will default.
- Should the group be 'open', with people coming as and when they want, or 'closed', with group members making a firm commitment to attend sessions? Open groups do function but there has to be some commitment to attendance or the group will never develop cohesion and trust.

- Should the group be compulsory? In our view it is preferable that everybody should attend, but in reality this is unlikely to happen. We recommend that new members of staff be expected to attend a number of group sessions to see whether this type of support is useful for them. It helps if they meet the group leader in advance. Many will choose to continue but some will not and making the group compulsory may undermine its effectiveness. However, if group support is not compulsory, those who do not attend may become suspicious of those who do. This makes it even more important that support is provided in a variety of ways so that members of staff can find support in ways that suit their needs at particular times.

Most staff when interviewed for a post in palliative care are sure that a group will be useful, even necessary. The reality is that, unless staff have experience of being a member of a group, they often find that it does not meet their needs. Quite soon they will find excuses to avoid it. When pressed to explain they say, 'I needed it last Friday when we were dealing with that difficult family'. It takes time to understand that the group's function is to help process the feelings experienced last Friday. Here is an example of how a support group can work.

A family, visiting their relative on the ward, are challenging and aggressive, questioning each procedure. As a result their primary nurse feels anxious and inadequate. He is able, up to a point, to check on the way he is responding with his colleagues and to share his worry. However, the ward is busy and there is little time to explore the way the situation with the family is affecting him. His support group provides a safe place to discuss his reactions and feelings and to discuss what might be happening within this family. It also provides an opportunity for other members to talk about how they deal with anger and to talk about similar situations.

During a group session there will be times when no one wants to speak and these may feel very uncomfortable. A skilled facilitator will help the group reflect on how silence affects us and how it allows people to identify their feelings so that they can be articulated. In this way the staff can be helped to see how important it is to let patients or relatives stay with silence.

Debriefing groups in special circumstances

Debriefing groups are needed from time to time following events that are likely to prove particularly traumatic to the staff. A suicide on a ward, the death of a staff member, a communal disaster or any other event that threatens the ability of the team to continue to function are all good reasons to hold such a meeting. It is often wise to choose someone from outside the team who is not closely involved and who has experience and training in debriefing. A psychiatrist or psychologist is likely to be of particular value for this purpose but there are also times when a senior manager is the best person to hold such a group (see page 184 for more details on debriefing).

Training

Education and training should be built into the work schedule. As well as increasing knowledge and developing skills, training provides time for reflection and processing.

Team building

More and more organizations are funding 'away days' for their staff, often focusing on team building or developing a corporate philosophy for their ward or primary care team.

Mentoring

It is increasingly common for nursing courses to require students to have a mentor, someone who is not a manager but who has nursing experience. Mentors need to be committed to offering support, sharing knowledge and encouraging reflective practice. Much will depend on the ability of the mentor and it is essential that mentors are provided with training and support. Successful mentoring rapidly develops both confidence and skills.

Supervision

Supervision, like mentoring, provides an opportunity for ongoing reflection. It gives people regular, legitimate opportunities to discuss how their work is affecting them, to reflect on their interactions with clients and to share their feelings of success or failure. Supervision is an essential part of counselling and social work practice. It should be a mandatory requirement for bereavement counsellors and it is appropriate that it is increasingly offered to home care nurses (in Britain these are often funded by the Macmillan Foundation and known as Macmillan nurses) and other hospital workers.

Supervision is best provided by someone who is trained in supervisory skills and has experience of the field. Supervisors usually work on a sessional basis, seeing people regularly, usually once or twice a month, with each session lasting about an hour. Ideally it should be offered on a one-to-one basis but group supervision can also be satisfactory provided numbers are kept small and adequate time is allowed (half an hour per person is a rough guide).

Supervision has three aspects:

* *Support and restoration.* By allowing people to reflect on how the work is affecting them the supervisor enables them to carry on caring for others. This helps people to monitor their case loads and resist overload. Although this may conflict with performance targets it is important for supervisors to help people to recognize when they are becoming overloaded and what is causing them to feel overloaded. If this is the result of personal or family illness or bereavement, the possibility of reducing the case load or granting a sabbatical should be considered. It is much easier to give volunteers time off than professionals. Supervision helps to maintain an awareness of personal needs among the demands of everyday work. It may well enable people to recognize their own need for counselling or for other measures of self-care and is important in preventing burn-out.
* *The ongoing development of skills.* The supervisor should enable workers to reflect on their interactions with their clients, examine how they are using their skills and how they are relating knowledge to practice. This enables them to carry on learning and is particularly important for people new to the work. It helps them to grapple with different ways of working and to gain confidence in their new environment.
* *Monitoring of the quality of the work and maintaining standards.* This includes ethical issues such as respecting confidentiality, maintaining appropriate boundaries (such as that between friendship and counselling) and demonstrating a respectful, non-judgemental attitude to clients.

Management also contains aspects of supervision. It is important to have agreed boundaries between line managers and supervisors. As supervision is concerned with accountability, some feedback will be required to the line manager. How this is handled needs to be negotiated and clarified for all parties from the outset. One way of providing such feedback is to link it to the appraisal process.

Management of the Team

Support, on its own, will not be sufficient to ensure that attention is given to the needs of the team. Naturally, as in any group, problems will arise, either within or between teams, and effective management of the multidisciplinary team, and of its sub-teams, is essential. Support will help staff deal with stresses and strains but it cannot compensate for poor management. It is not in the remit of this book to describe management practices. It is important, however, to remember that the way in which the manager deals with tensions or problems arising within the team will have a vital impact on its ability to provide effective care. Senior staff should listen to the opinions of their junior colleagues and, if they disagree, say why. It is much easier to tolerate disagreement if there is mutual respect and affection than if staff ignore each other's needs.

Management of care is usually shared by senior members of staff. Each must be aware of his or her own particular areas of responsibility and meet regularly. Increasingly, in the UK, this group will have responsibility for the budget of their unit. Financial constraints can introduce another philosophy to the three outlined at the start of this chapter. Sadly it is seldom the case that 'cheapest is best'.

Good management, working with a mentor, supervision, appraisal and access to a peer support group are all part of a framework for developing sound, safe practice for the families receiving our care.

The Setting in which Care Takes Place

At various times patients who are approaching the end of their lives will be cared for at home, in hospital wards and in hospices. Their family may also receive help from services for the bereaved. In concluding this chapter we shall say a little about each of these settings, the special characteristics of each and the advantages and disadvantages of the setting for the people who work in them, as well as for the families they serve.

Caring at home

Three things are needed if people are to be cared for at home: a patient whose physical and emotional symptoms can be controlled, a family who are willing and able to cope with the demands of the situation, and a team of professionals who have the necessary skills and are available at all times of the day or night. Given these, most patients can remain at home and will often opt to die there. If, however, any of these things is missing, admission to a hospital or hospice will have to be considered. This should not be seen as a failure but as an appropriate part of any integrated programme of care.

Although, most of the time, most patients feel more secure in their own homes, surrounded by their own families, than they do in hospital, the same cannot be said for the professionals who visit them. Nurses, general practitioners (GPs) and other professionals are usually on their own when visiting the family. They have to make decisions without consulting their colleagues, have no immediate back-up and, by comparison with hospital staff, little opportunity of keeping a close watch on the patient. This makes it all the more important for the members of the team to meet frequently and to support each other. The work requires a special kind of person who is confident enough to enjoy making decisions on their own and able to tolerate and mitigate the family's anxiety. They must be self-reliant but able to accept help when it is needed and to recognize the need.

The primary care team is normally best placed to provide continuity of care for seriously ill patients, who are often being passed from one hospital department to another. With any luck they already know the patient and may be well acquainted with the family. This gives them background knowledge and an ongoing relationship of trust, which can be of great value to patients and their families. It is also of value to the team, who have much more confidence in their ability to handle the situation if they know the people involved. The flip side of this coin, however, is the pain which the primary team must suffer when people whom they have known for years are dying or in great distress.

Carole, who was 19 years of age and planning to marry in a few months, developed cramp-like abdominal pains. She agreed with her family doctor that they were probably attributable to stress. Her parents' marriage was foundering and she was anxious about leaving home at this time to get married. Eventually the pain became intolerable and further investigations were instituted. The house surgeon and primary care nurse on the ward to which she was admitted both knew about the family stress, so Carole assumed that the GP had referred to it in his letter to the hospital.

When a malignant tumour was diagnosed Carole felt angry and frightened. She blamed her GP for missing the diagnosis and for causing the hospital staff to see her as a 'psychiatric case'. The hospital informed her GP, who visited her in hospital. He made no attempt to justify himself but said openly and frankly, 'I'm sorry, Carole, I was barking up the wrong tree.' This apology restored her faith in the doctor and helped to set down roots in their relationship which then continued to nourish and support her until she died, four years later.

The problem of maintaining a satisfactory liaison with specialist staff is considerable and, while everyone pays lip service to the importance of communication, this remains the commonest thing to go wrong. Lack of consultation between teams, delays in passing on information and the particular difficulties of working together to provide consistent psychological support give rise to endless problems and make it most important for the primary care team to monitor what is happening.

Specialist home care teams, which may include nurses, social workers and doctors, are a valuable adjunct to the primary care team and can provide expertise which this team lacks. It is often tempting for them to take over main responsibility for care but, if they do this, the primary care team will learn nothing and may resent the intrusion and stop using their services. Home care teams, therefore, have the difficult job of relating, on the one hand, to the family who are doing most of the caring and, on the other, to the primary care team, who need to remain involved in all significant issues. This seriously limits their power and, while great things can be achieved if there is sufficient trust and goodwill, difficulties will often arise. For this reason and because of all the other stresses of the work, the specialist home care team need to make time to support each other as well as to liaise about the families under their care. It is important for doctors who work with the team to be part of the support network and to give this the priority that it needs. Too often they assume that discussions with nurses should always be patient-focused and fail to give proper attention to discussing the family, the team itself and the relationship of the team to the other primary and secondary carers who are involved.

Psychologists and others with special skills in group counselling and support can be of considerable value to all who are caring for people who are facing death, bereavement and other transitions. Their roles will be discussed in more detail on page 135.

Hospital care

Ward care suits professional staff who like to work in a close-knit unit, do not mind being told what to do and enjoy close relationships with their patients. In home care it is the family who remain the main source of succour to the patient, while in the hospital it is the nurse. Because the patient is present all the time and the family members come and go, nurses' relationships with their patients tends to be closer than their relationships with the patients' families. They tend to see the patient as 'my patient' and this sometimes gives rise to rivalry with the family. Most often the family defer to the nurse's claims and take a back seat, even when it might be more appropriate for them to share in the caring.

Most hospital wards contain a mixture of patients who require different philosophies of care and it is, therefore, hard to create the kind of supportive environment that is possible at home or in a hospice. This is nowhere more obvious than it is on a radiotherapy or oncology ward, where some patients are receiving curative treatment, some will be left with lasting disabilities and others will die. Only too often patients for whom there is a chance of cure are given priority over those who are seen as 'hopeless cases'. The patient and staff may believe that 'nothing can be done' and staff may even resent the patient who is 'blocking a bed' which might otherwise be used more profitably.

Attitudes such as this can make it very hard for the staff member who understands what is needed but feels unsupported by other members of the team. We cannot over-emphasize the importance of counteracting this tendency and it is the responsibility of the senior staff to see that patients who require a rehabilitative or palliative care orientation receive the type of care that is appropriate and do not feel rejected.

The creation of specialist nursing posts aimed at meeting the special needs of patients who require rehabilitation (such as the mastectomy nurse or colostomy nurse) or palliative care (such as the palliative care nurse[2]) helps to redress the balance, since these nurses not only provide direct help to patients and families but also orientate and instruct the other members of the ward team. They also have an important liaison role when the patient goes home or moves into another unit. While these nurses have an important function in support of the front line of ward staff they need to seek elsewhere for their own support. This will come most naturally from other staff who adopt the same orientation as themselves but this may be difficult in small hospitals, where there may be only one or two similar staff.

Other staff who have important roles to play in hospital settings include social workers, physiotherapists, chaplains, occupational therapists, psychologists and doctors. Like the specialist nurses, they each have dual allegiance, to the ward team and to their own professional teams, but it may well be that neither of these teams adopts a philosophy of care that is appropriate to all of the patients whom the staff are called upon to treat. It is, therefore, worth considering a third type of team, which is a multidisciplinary group of people who share a common philosophy of care. Thus regular meetings of all those hospital staff who are engaged in palliative care and need to support each other can be very valuable.

Hospice care

Hospices in Britain originated as residential units and added home care and day care only at a later date. In the USA, many hospices provide only home care. In this chapter we use 'hospice' in its original sense: a specialist unit which provides residential as well as other care for people with life-threatening illness for which active treatment is no longer appropriate. Many of the patients admitted to such units will die there, although there are others who may be admitted for symptom control or respite care before returning home. There are also some hospices that admit patients requiring

---

2 In some settings, the hospital palliative care nurse doubles as a home care nurse, thereby ensuring good liaison between hospital and home. This is possible only if the patient lives in the locality of the hospital.

long-term care, such as for motor neurone disease, and for whom the main object is to maintain or restore autonomy.

Many of the issues discussed above in the provision of care in hospital apply equally to care in a hospice. There are, however, some differences that deserve separate consideration. Much of the success of hospices arises from their whole-hearted adoption of the philosophy of palliative care for all patients who come to them. But this may not always be appropriate. Thus, not every patient admitted to a hospice is suitable for a palliative philosophy of care, and rehabilitation is often more appropriate. Again it is most important for staff to recognize the difference if patients with rehabilitation needs are not to be overshadowed by those who are dying.

Colin had been in the hospice for a month when the staff began to complain about his 'attention-seeking behaviour'. He had been admitted for long-term care of motor neurone disease that had paralysed his arms and legs and left him unable to look after himself at home. Although his ultimate prognosis was poor he was certainly not near to death and the physiotherapists instituted a programme aimed at making him as independent as possible. Nurses were advised not to do anything that he could do for himself, and to encourage autonomy.

Colin, who had not understood the plan, felt that he was being neglected. He noticed how attentive the nurses were to the needs of patients who were dying and who were being 'waited on hand and foot' and he concluded that 'We MND patients are second-class citizens'. He responded by adopting an assertive and demanding attitude to the staff, who began to resent his criticisms. This conflict seriously undermined his relationships with the people on whom he was going to depend for the rest of his life.

This case illustrates well the type of problem that can arise when more than one philosophy of care is being adopted on the same ward. It may be that Colin would have been happier in a unit dedicated solely to rehabilitation, but there was also a lot that could be done to reduce the misunderstandings by helping him and the staff to clarify their own roles and relationships.

In the end the success or failure of a unit to give satisfactory care depends upon the resources available. If we accept that psycho-social and spiritual care are a proper part of the philosophy of palliative care, then it is important for staff to have the training and the time to provide these. Hospices may not need to spend money on high-tech medicine but they do need to spend it on staff. One can only imagine the kind of death house that might result if hospices were to be set up without sufficient staff to provide this care. Sadly there are some settings in which this nightmare is already beginning to occur.

Given the staff that are needed, is it realistic to imagine that they can truly provide people with the kind of emotional support that those at home can expect to get from their families? Research at St Christopher's Hospice in Sydenham suggests that it is. Relatives of patients who had died in that hospice were compared with relatives of patients who had died in other hospitals in the locality. They were asked whether they agreed or disagreed with each of a list of statements characterizing the hospital (or hospice) in question. Statements such as 'Nothing is too much trouble' and 'Don't worry' were commonly checked for both settings. The statement that best distinguished hospice from hospital care was 'The hospital (or hospice) is like a family'. This was agreed by 78% of those whose relative had died in the hospice and 11% of those whose relative died elsewhere (Parkes, 1979). Recent research confirms these findings (Seale, 1996).

The rapid growth of the hospice movement is a success story which reflects the disillusionment felt by many of those who have witnessed the consequences of inappropriate care for people who are dying; but it is in danger of becoming a victim of its own success. The idealized view of hospice care may satisfy society's need for reassurance that it is possible to take away all of the pain and misery of terminal illness. Unfortunately it leaves the professionals who work in hospices (who may have been attracted to the work by this adulation) with the problem of reconciling expectations with reality. Clearly, any job satisfaction must relate to reasonable rather than idealized expectations and it is important for those who recruit and train staff to work in such settings not to collude with cant.

Despite these misperceptions, the morale of hospice staff is usually no worse and is often higher than that of professionals working in other settings. Much depends on the system of support for staff, which needs to be intrinsic and continuous. Staff support is not the responsibility of one person but of everyone. We should strive for the kind of mutual support that is provided by a good family.

Bereavement Services

Although the philosophy of care required by bereaved families comes closer to that of rehabilitation than palliative care, none of the preceding models is entirely appropriate, because the majority of bereaved people are not sick. They may, for a while, feel weak, helpless and disabled by grief, but it is seldom helpful and may be harmful for those who give care to think of them as in need of 'therapy'. Bereaved people who come to think of themselves as sick easily become dependent on those who adopt the role of therapist.

This means that those doctors and nurses who choose to provide care to the bereaved need to be careful not to treat bereaved people as 'patients'. This is so much at variance with our habitual roles that it requires special training to bring home its implications. Those who do not have this training may do better to limit their care to the assessment of risk and the provision of information and to leave it to specialist bereavement counsellors or mutual help organizations to provide extra care for the minority who need it.

Specialist counsellors themselves need to be careful not to model themselves on therapists. This may be difficult when psycho-therapists, psychiatrists and clinical psychologists are used to train counsellors. They need to be aware of the dangers of medicalizing normal life crises and to be clear that bereavement counselling is a preventive rather than a curative activity.

In Britain the majority of those who become bereavement counsellors are not members of the caring professions. Most are volunteers who have been selected and trained to adopt a philosophy of care which sees grief as a process of growth or development which, if it proceeds in a satisfactory way, will end in the person becoming stronger, wiser and more mature than they were before the bereavement. Counselling may be needed to help provide the secure base from which the bereaved can begin the painful process of accepting what is gone and discovering what can now be used to fashion a new direction in life.

Although some bereavement counsellors work as a team to provide help to individuals, families or groups of bereaved people (see Chapters 3, 6 and 7 for details) most bereavement counselling is one-to-one, with a single counsellor visiting or being visited by a single bereaved person. Like the visiting nurse, they need to be able to work on their own and need the support of a team of fellow counsellors and a supervisor who will provide the support that they are providing to their clients.

Summary

❑ Care aimed at cure, care aimed at rehabilitation and palliative care require us to adopt different philosophies of care. Medical and nursing teams often fail to meet the needs of patients or their families because they have adopted a philosophy of care that is inappropriate to the circumstances. Cure-orientated care is patient-focused and time limited. It expects little change in the life of the patient or family.

❑ In rehabilitation-orientated care the aim is to help patients to achieve the maximum possible autonomy. To achieve this patients and their families may need to grieve for what they are losing.

❑ Palliative care has two aims, to relieve symptoms and to support transition in patients and their families. Involvement with the family is essential and power should be shared. Responsibility may need to change and reside at various times with the patient, the family and the team.

❑ Changing from one philosophy of care to another is often needed and is difficult for patient, family members and staff. Staff need to be clear in their own minds which philosophy they are adopting and to communicate this to the patient and family with tact and sensitivity.

❑ Although not all families need our care and others will refuse it, we do have a responsibility to reach out to the family, to find out who they are, assess their needs and make clear to them our willingness to become involved and to support them.

❑ Normally the needs of patients will take priority but, in the long term, it is important to meet the needs of staff as well as those of patients and their families.

❑ It is important to distinguish staff grief from staff burn-out. Grief is normal, transient and draws staff members together in mutual support. Burn-out is chronic, insidious and infectious. It undermines teams and may drive people out of the caring professions. Every effort must be made to prevent it and to intervene as soon as it is detected. Burn-out is not a psychiatric illness but it can increase the risk of one.

❑ There is no one method of staff support that will meet the needs of all people: a network of formal and informal support is required and staff should be free to choose what suits them best.

❑ Specialist nursing posts aimed at meeting the special needs of patients who require rehabilitation or palliative care enables direct help to be given to patients and families and to orientate and instruct the other members of the ward team. They may also liaise with the primary care team when the patient is discharged.

❑ Hospices provide specialist palliative care but may find difficulty in adopting a rehabilitative philosophy when this is more appropriate.

❑ It is seldom helpful and may be harmful for those who give care to families after bereavement to think of them as in need of 'therapy'. Bereavement counselling is a preventive rather than a curative activity.

3

Counselling

This chapter outlines the skills involved in providing effective support to people facing death and bereavement. We begin by defining what we mean by counselling and counselling skills.

We argue that working in this field demands that helpers, both professional and volunteer, be proficient in the use of counselling skills. We describe the principles of counselling, the core components of establishing effective relationships, and interpersonal and counselling skills. Finally we highlight issues that are particular to counselling dying and bereaved people.

What Do We Mean by Counselling?

The word 'counselling' has many meanings. Like other books in this series we use a broad definition which encompasses any situation in which the focus of a relationship is that one person is attempting to help another. The essence of counselling is in the manner of helping. When we use the word we mean that the helper is listening to and communicating with the other person in a purposeful way – in a way that is enabling, whether it involves helping other people make decisions about their care or whether it is focused on exploring how they are reacting to their present predicament. The aim is usually to help the other person to feel valued, respected and resourceful, the more so if horizons are limited by disease.

Counselling in Palliative Care

In our experience the majority of patients and relatives seldom seek formal counselling from qualified counsellors but many want to talk over their circumstances with their professional carers. Consequently in palliative care, counselling usually takes place within the context of a relationship which is primarily focused on non-counselling activities. As a result relatively few health care professionals see themselves as 'counsellors' even though they frequently use the core counselling skills. Because this type of counselling takes place within a wider context, some aspects of formal counselling, such as putting aside separate time, or negotiating the duration and frequency of sessions, or even being able to ensure privacy on a hospital ward, may be difficult to put into practice and may even be inappropriate.

In palliative care we are working with people who are faced with enormous changes in their lives. They have much to say about their hopes and fears, about what it is like to be ill and what sense they make of illness and the situations in which they find themselves. Arthur Frank (a Canadian sociologist), speaking from his personal experience of heart disease and cancer, vividly describes the need to talk not only about what is happening to the physical body, what he calls 'disease talk', but also to talk about the experience of living with critical illness, which he calls 'illness talk'.

> Illness is the experience of living through the disease. If disease talk measures the body, illness talk tells of the fear and frustration of being inside a body that is breaking down. Illness begins where medicine leaves off, where I recognise that what is happening to my body is not some set of measures. What happens to my body happens to my life. My life consists of temperature and circulation, but also of hopes and disappointments, joys and sorrows, none of which can be measured. In illness talk there is no such thing as *the* body, only *my* body as I experience it. Disease talk charts the progression of certain measures. Illness talk is a story about moving from a perfectly comfortable body to one that forces me to ask: What is happening to me? Not *it*, but *me*.
>
> (Frank, 1991: 13)

Frank found that few health care professionals were prepared to engage in 'illness talk'. He suggests that this was partly a consequence of the multiple demands made on health care professionals that so often place such sharing beyond the boundaries of 'professional' activity. The main reason, however, seemed to be that professional carers avoided such conversations because they were too embarrassing and difficult. This forces patients into silence. As Frank says:

> A person who finds no one willing to take the time and offer the help necessary to bring forth speech will protect himself by saying nothing. But the time when I cannot immediately put something into words is usually the time when I most need to express myself.... The problem is finding someone who will help you work out the terms of that expression.
>
> (Frank 1991: 14)

Sharing the experience of illness helps patients and their caregivers come to terms with the impact of critical illness. It helps remove feelings of isolation and reduces anxiety and fear. In other words, health care professionals need to be able to help patients and relatives share their experiences and 'tell their story'. This way of working with people, to listen in a way that is enabling and empowering, is central to counselling.

The following examples illustrate common situations where counselling skills can help us respond to patients and enable them to share their concerns.

Mary, a district nurse, was visiting Susan, a young woman with ovarian cancer, to set up a syringe driver to control her nausea and vomiting. Susan was lying on her bed with the bedroom door open so that her young children could come in and out to see what the nurse was doing to their mother. In a quiet moment Susan suddenly asked fearfully, 'How long do you think I've got?' Mary could have assumed that Susan was asking 'How long have I got to go on using this syringe driver?' but she felt that Susan was saying 'How long have I got before I die?' She could have deflected this question by professing ignorance. Instead Mary met Susan's eyes and tentatively explored whether she was expressing her fears about her uncertain future and her concerns for her children. She accepted Susan's sadness and showed by her genuine concern that it was all right to talk about these painful feelings. Mary went away feeling sad and helpless but, by talking about her feelings and reflecting on her responses with her colleagues, felt reassured that she had responded appropriately. Susan now knew that Mary cared about her and was prepared to take the time to listen. She felt less isolated and that her situation was a little more manageable.

Jim, a nurse, was on night duty and was settling Mr Cartwright down for the night. As he leaned over the bed to turn out the light Mr Cartwright clutched his arm and whispered, 'Can there really be a God, Jim?' We can imagine some of Jim's thoughts. 'Heavens, I'm not a bit religious. Where the hell do I find a chaplain at this time of night?' He could have muttered, 'I think God knows best,' and escaped to another patient. What he did was to draw up a chair and hold Mr Cartwright's hand between his and reply, 'I don't know; it's hard to believe sometimes isn't it?' Mr Cartwright closed his eyes and drifted off to sleep. Jim sat beside him for a few minutes thinking about the loneliness of dying and the apparent meaningless of learning so much in a lifetime only to die at the end.

Dr Gwen Jones was finishing evening surgery, thankfully, when the receptionist buzzed through that Mr Simmonds was in reception without an appointment and wondered if the doctor would see him for five minutes. With a lurch of her heart Gwen recalled that David Simmonds had mesothelioma, had not responded well to treatment and was difficult to talk to because of his aggressive manner. Gwen knew that she had put off visiting because she did not know how to deal with David's anger. Gwen was tired, hungry and wanted to get home to see her children. Her first thought was to tell David that the time had come to involve the hospice; after all, the staff there were used to counselling and dealing with anger. As David entered she was ready with a prepared line but David sat down heavily and put his head in his hands. Gwen felt the weight of the man's despair and heard herself say, 'You look like you've reached the end of your tether, David.' Together they sat in silence for several minutes. Slowly and painfully David told her of the pain and nausea he was experiencing, that he could only sleep after half a bottle of whisky, that his wife was drinking like a fish too, and that he wished he was dead and out of it. Gwen conveyed that she had heard and understood by repeating back in her own words David's list of apparently insoluble problems and then explained what she as a doctor could do to help and suggested who else could be involved. David agreed to a referral to the hospice team in the knowledge that Gwen would continue to see him. He went away feeling lighter and less despairing about his situation. Gwen went home feeling that the 15 minutes she had spent with David had probably been the most useful of the day. She had found herself, jet lagged as she was with caring and listening all day, genuinely involved and able to respond empathically. It felt right to involve the hospice, not as a last resort but because she had taken the time to listen to what was really concerning her patient.

The professionals in these examples were using counselling skills or working in a counselling mode rather than 'counselling'. They responded to the patients' concerns as they arose, recognizing that what was wanted was a relationship that would help them *explore what was happening* and *voice their feelings.* On the surface it can be very difficult to draw a clear distinction between counselling and using counselling skills. In our first example, Mary could have gone on to work with Susan in a counselling mode over a period of time. An outside observer listening to their conversations would find it hard to tell the difference between what Mary was doing and what a trained Counsellor would have done, with the exception that Mary would also be attending to Susan's physical needs. A crucial difference is that neither Mary nor Susan perceived that what was taking place was counselling. It was seen as the provision of support, a natural part of Mary's professional caring role. So the difference between counselling and the use of counselling skills lies in the level of training and understanding of the practitioners, the focus of their role and in the understanding of the recipient. It is obviously of great benefit to patients and relatives if the professionals caring for them are skilled and confident in a range of ways of helping. The danger lies in the potential conflict between the different roles and in not being aware of the limits of our competence.

In health care, working in a counselling mode is one of a range of ways of providing appropriate care.

The Spectrum of Helping Strategies

It is useful to view helping as a spectrum of possible ways of responding (Fig. 3.1). At one end of the spectrum are the ways of helping people in which the professional is more in control. These strategies, such as taking direct action, and giving advice, information and reassurance, are frequently used in situations where professionals have specialist knowledge and fit the general ethos of the health service. At the other end of the spectrum are strategies in which the client has greater control and the professional plays a

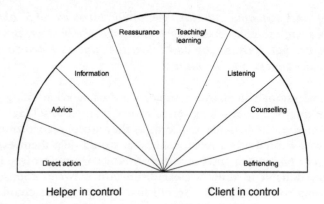

Helper in control   Client in control

Figure 3.1   A spectrum of helping strategies.

more enabling role. These include counselling and befriending. The meaning of most of these terms is self-evident but it is worth pointing out that giving reassurance is seldom successful unless information is given at the same time. Patients are not reassured if the doctor pats them on the head and tells them not to worry.

The term 'befriending' is here used with a special meaning. We use it to indicate a type of caring aimed at meeting the client's emotional, social or practical needs. It has more elements of sharing and reciprocity than does counselling and is more open ended. Befriending is less focused and, although it may be time limited, it often continues for a considerable length of time. Some bereavement support groups set out to provide this kind of help.

In palliative care all of these strategies are used at different times, depending on the needs of the client, the skill of the helper and the scope of the helper's role. It would be unlikely, for example, that professionals would act as befrienders, but they may pass on information about patient support groups, good neighbour schemes and so on. We cannot be fully effective as carers if we concentrate on one or two strategies. For example, we may be superb listeners but unless we are prepared to share our knowledge of what is available in the community we can deny patients and families access to practical help. We may need to provide access to financial help, enable the home to be altered so that a patient can use a wheelchair, or involve the school in providing help for the children.

Fundamental to all the helping strategies is the ability to assess the patient's needs and we cannot do this without effective interpersonal skills. Communication skills such as listening, exploring, clarifying and responding are the common core and are often referred to as basic counselling skills. These will be explored later in the chapter.

Specialist Counselling

It is clear that those caring for the terminally ill and bereaved need to have specialist skills in order to respond to the everyday situations they encounter. There are times when the added skills of a specialist Counsellor are also needed. These are, or should be, highly skilled professionals who have completed a lengthy training course, including the theory of psychological and social functioning, and a period of supervised practice. They may be skilled in group work and family work as well as in working one to one. In palliative care they may work directly with patients or families, focusing on those people who have complex relationship problems or psychological needs. They also have much to offer other staff. They may help others develop their basic skills and can provide support and insight derived from their training and experience. Although we can make a distinction between the work of specialist Counsellors and other health care professionals, it is important to remember that they use the same counselling skills.

There are a number of schools of counselling and psychotherapy, not all of which are appropriate to the dying and the bereaved. Indeed, at a specialist level it can be hard to distinguish counselling from psychotherapy. Those of particular relevance to this field include person-centred counselling, gestalt counselling, art therapy, logotherapy, family therapy, crisis intervention, stress management, cognitive therapy, rational–emotive therapy and pastoral counselling. Each of these has something special to offer, and together they present us with confusing choices. There is a fair amount of overlap between the different schools and the differences are more often of emphasis than of principle. Rather than over-simplifying these issues by attempting to delineate the differences, we shall refer to some of the lessons to be learned from particular schools at various points in this book. For ourselves, we prefer to adopt an eclectic model, drawing our ideas from several schools rather than identifying ourselves with only one. In practice, our readers will need to find out what is available in their own area, meet the people involved and draw their own conclusions.

No mention has been made of the major schools of Freudian, Jungian and other psychodynamic therapies. These have all been developed to treat mental illness and they may be of help to the minority of bereaved people who develop major psychiatric disorders. Counsellors are more concerned with the prevention of psychiatric disorders than their treatment. Those who require such treatment should be referred to psychiatrists rather than to Counsellors, and their care lies beyond the scope of this volume.

The Principles of Counselling

Whether or not counselling is being offered in the context of a wider role or by a Counsellor, the following principles should be considered.

*   Counselling should be practised within a recognized *code of ethics*. This should include maintaining confidentiality (see pages 68–69) as well as other issues.[1]
*   It should be *focused* and have specific goals.
*   It should *move towards the clients' autonomy*, allowing them to gain more control over the situation they are facing.
*   It should be *time limited*. In palliative care the progression of disease imposes limits to our contact with patients. When working with bereaved people, however, the duration of contact needs to be made clear.
*   It should be a *one-way relationship*. The helper's personal experiences should be shared only if there is a purpose for so doing. Each person is unique and talking about our own experiences may appear dismissive or cause clients to judge themselves against our standards.

Usha, a bereavement counsellor, was asked by her client, a widower with a three-year-old son, whether she was a widow. She replied that she was and continued to answer her client's questions, revealing that she had been widowed when pregnant. Her client responded, 'You must think I'm a real wimp to be reacting the way I am.' It took all Usha's skill to rebuild trust so that the relationship could continue. Refusing to reveal anything

---

1   The British Association of Counselling (1993) has specified codes of ethics for the practice of counselling and for supervision.

about ourselves can, on the other hand, make us appear one dimensional, cold and distant.

- Counselling should involve explicit agreement that the client is *working towards change*. This may appear difficult, as we cannot bring about the changes most desired by our clients – we cannot prevent the patient from dying nor return the dead to life. We can, however, help people change their perception. We can help people feel less isolated and hopeless, as described in our examples on pages 52 and 53.
- It should be supported by a learning environment in which it is expected that *skills will be acquired and practised*. Opportunities for further education and training should be built into the workload.
- It should be *supervised*. The value of supervision is now being recognized by those working with the dying and the bereaved. Some families evoke deep and confusing feelings in us. When this happens it helps to discuss, and reflect on, the situation. Training and experience may enhance our understanding but do not protect us from suffering. Sooner or later we are likely to find ourselves brought to a halt by our own or our colleague's reactions. The people for whom we are caring may suffer if we do not reflect on our work and examine our motives. Time for reflection must be built into the work. Ways of doing this were discussed in Chapter 2.

The Counselling Relationship

When asked to describe what helps at times of crisis or difficulty, most people will talk about being listened to, feeling understood, and being accepted as themselves and not criticized or judged. This approach is central to the non-directive or 'client-centred' school of counselling founded by Carl Rogers. This style of counselling is rooted in the belief in the individual's capacity for growth and self-realization when provided with an enabling relationship (Rogers, 1951).

The three fundamental components of non-directive counselling reflect this attitude. The first component is the capacity to *respect* others and to accept them non-judgementally. The second is *empathy* – the ability accurately to perceive feelings that the other person is experiencing without being overwhelmed by them. This capacity to enter the feeling world of the other and to convey understanding of that world is called empathic listening. The third, often called *genuineness*, is to be ourselves. This encompasses accepting ourselves, knowing our personal limits and understanding how our own experiences may affect our responses.

The combination of these three components enables *the development of trust and safety* so that difficult feelings can be shared and new perspectives gained.

Respect

The aim is to convey our belief that each person is worthwhile, unique and valuable. We can convey our respect for others by:

*   introducing ourselves by name and explaining what our role is;
*   finding out how the client wishes to be addressed (we should not assume that people wish to be known by their first name);
*   remembering names;
*   saying how much time is available;
*   giving undivided attention;
*   listening;
*   not interrupting or talking over;
*   not making snap judgements or being critical;
*   checking our assumptions;
*   encouraging clients to make their own decisions rather than assuming that we know best.

Empathy

Empathy involves being able to sense accurately and appreciate another person's reality and to convey that understanding sensitively. Rogers defines empathic listening in the following way:

> It means entering the private perceptual world of the other and becoming thoroughly at home in it. It involves being sensitive, moment by moment, to the changing meanings which flow in this other person, to the fear or rage or tenderness or confusion or whatever, that he or she is experiencing. It means temporarily living in the other's life, moving about in it delicately without making judgements. It's a way of saying 'I'm with you, I've been listening carefully to what you've been saying and expressing and I'm checking to see if my understanding is accurate.'
>
> (Rogers, 1975)

Empathy does *not* mean losing our objectivity to the point that we share our clients' misperceptions about themselves and their world. Many people see the world as hostile and themselves as helpless; if we see them in the same way we become of little use to them. We convey empathy by:

- reflecting back the feelings that we are picking up from the other person;
- mirroring the behaviour of the other person, for example by smiling when the other person smiles (unconsciously rather than in a contrived way).

Genuineness

The aim is to be ourselves in the relationship and thereby convey that we have a genuine concern and can be trusted. Being oneself means knowing ourselves and our limits. It does not mean putting aside our role as a doctor, social worker or nurse but being ourselves within that role. We convey that we are genuine by:

- responding naturally;
- not pretending to be someone that we are not;
- talking *appropriately* about our own feelings and beliefs;
- being spontaneous;
- making sure that our expressions and bodily gestures are congruent with what we are saying;
- not being defensive.

The combination of these three basic attitudes to others enables the development of a trusting relationship in which it feels safe enough to share difficult feelings.

These attitudes are insufficient on their own, however. They must be *conveyed* if the patient or carer is to feel understood. This involves effective communication skills, the core skills of helping relationships.

Counselling Skills

Counselling in part involves using more purposefully the communication skills that all of us have built up from the day of our birth. Considering how to improve communication usually feels very uncomfortable, as it causes us to worry about all the times when we may have been making mistakes or 'getting it wrong'. Improving our skills means becoming aware of all our unconscious ways of being with others, so it is not surprising that we usually go through a period of feeling deskilled and self-conscious in our interactions with others. But these feeling of self-consciousness fade as the new techniques become internalized and the end result is likely to be a major improvement in both skills and confidence. We cannot improve our ability to work with others solely by reading about counselling skills – we must practise. What follows, therefore, should be regarded as an aid to training and not an alternative.

Active listening

Listening is fundamental to all helping relationships. It is often assumed that because listening is part of everyday communication, it is a skill that we do not need to practise or improve. Communication in everyday life is, however, fraught with misunderstanding and we often fail to understand each other. It is common to hear people say, 'I didn't really mean that,' or 'You don't understand what I mean,' and worrying about whether one said the right thing is a familiar experience.

The ability to communicate is an essential component of counselling. Communication may be verbal or non-verbal and may focus on thoughts or feelings. In order to be able to understand what other people are trying to tell us we must listen to all these elements, not just to the words. This demands giving people our total attention. It is not a passive process but an active engagement. It requires the use of all our senses. It means listening with our ears to what is being said and to the tone of voice, listening with our minds to understand the message contained in the words, listening with our eyes to what is being conveyed through the client's posture, bearing and gestures, and listening with our hearts to the human being we are trying to understand. Listening in this way enables clients to feel that we are really there with them and value who they are. Receiving attention from another person is the first need that all of us share from the first moment of life. As Arthur Frank described, the need for attention becomes acutely pertinent as the end of life approaches. Erikson (1964) described the effect of both inattention and negative attention on the child:

Hardly has one learned to recognise the familiar face when one becomes frightfully aware of the unfamiliar, the strange face, the unresponsive, the averted and the frowning face. And here begins the inexplicable tendency on man's part to feel that he has caused the face to turn away.

(Erikson, 1964)

When we are vulnerable we become acutely aware of other people's attitudes to us and will often decide that an averted face is a signal of an averted heart. The behaviour of the doctor who does not take her eyes off the computer screen on her desk when talking to a patient or of the person who crosses the road in order to avoid meeting a bereaved person will usually be interpreted as uninterest and rejection.

Obstacles to active listening

Many things can distract us from giving others our full attention, particularly on a busy ward. It is important to consider what may block our ability to listen.

External distractions. We can be distracted by external factors such as noise, and our awareness of other patients, of other tasks waiting to be completed, and of the expectations of our colleagues. It can be hard to give attention when we know that we are needed to help with another patient, or should be in a meeting. If we are working with people in their own homes, children may be playing in an adjacent room or the television may be on. In these situations we have to do the best we can to screen out the external distractions. If the intention is to raise a sensitive issue or impart distressing information, we should try to minimize potential distractions by, for example, setting aside sufficient time, moving into a quiet room and creating as much privacy as the environment allows.

Internal distractions. We can also be distracted by internal factors. We may find our ability to listen is compromised by the common tendency in conversations to make assumptions about what the other person is saying. In everyday interactions it is quite usual for listeners to switch their attention on and off, to get distracted by what they think about what the other person is saying and rehearse their reply. It is easy to listen with the ears but not with the mind, to listen selectively and jump to conclusions about what the speaker is saying because we have heard it before. This is especially easy to do if we are feeling pressured and is not helped by the fact that we think much more quickly than we speak. When this is happening there is a great temptation to interrupt the speaker, but we should do this only if the conversation starts to ramble or we are being overwhelmed by too much detail.

Engaging in conversations with terminally ill or bereaved people can arouse powerful feelings of helplessness and anxiety about our competence to respond sensitively. Many people are drawn to health care as a profession because they want to be able to make others feel better. When much of our training is about what we can do to improve a situation, it can be hard to believe that sensitive listening is sufficient. As we said earlier, active listening requires us not to 'do' but to 'be', and this can feel very uncomfortable.

Talking to terminally ill or bereaved people may also arouse memories of our own painful experiences or evoke feelings of insecurity as we confront mortality. It is common to become fearful for the wellbeing of those we love, and to imagine what it would be like for our families and friends if we were to die. These feelings may cause us to switch our attention off what our client is saying on to ourselves, or may prevent us from engaging in a conversation that is painful for us.

Our ability to listen is also influenced by our own background and culture. Our life experience creates filters through which we sift and place all that we hear. It can be hard to accept and empathize with people who seem very different from ourselves, or whose way of coping is the opposite of our own. Differences in value systems, race, culture, gender, education, use of vocabulary or class background can block our ability to hear what the other person is saying. Conversely, identifying someone as similar to us and sharing our values and way of life can prevent us from listening to what they are trying to communicate.

We are all familiar with loss and it is impossible for our own reactions and responses not to affect the way we respond to others facing major loss and change. It is important to develop our awareness of our personal filters and the effects of our own experience of loss so that we can understand how our attitudes and prejudices may affect our responses to others. If we have awareness we can check our assumptions, share our reactions with colleagues and know when we need to seek guidance.

Distractions may be expressed through body language. An open posture, sitting down at the same level as the client and maintaining gentle eye contact conveys the willingness to listen. Crossed arms and legs and remaining standing (particularly if the other person is in bed) convey an unwillingness to engage. Facial expression is also important. A young house officer (internist) admitted that the more despairing she felt about the information she had to impart, the more she felt a stiff smile slap itself on her face. At some time early on in life, she had learnt to smile to disguise her feelings. She realized that she needed to explore what had caused her to create this self-protective barrier that prevented patients and those close to them from expressing fear and anxiety.

Concentrating on the facts and trying to remember the whole history can also get in the way of active listening. Although making one or two notes at the end of a conversation may be helpful, trying to write it all down while the other person is talking will inevitably make it more difficult to listen to what the person is actually saying and may cause the other person to be inhibited. If the other person feels that we are mainly interested in the facts rather than their experience it will be hard to develop trust and openness.

Listening to non-verbal messages

At times clients will give conflicting messages. Their behaviour may convey something different from what they are saying verbally. For example, if a patient responds to your question, 'Is there anything making you feel uncomfortable?' by clenching her fists and turning her head away while saying, 'No, I'm fine,' you would be right to doubt her verbal denial.

Active listening, striving to understand others, is quite different from ordinary conversation. It is an art that demands giving full attention to the other person while also being aware of our own reactions. It is as demanding of energy as physical work. However, the willingness to listen is the key to all helping relationships.

We demonstrate our support and willingness to understand not only by listening but by the ways in which we respond.

Encouragement

The client may need encouragement and a reminder that you are still listening. Maintaining gentle eye contact, nodding, smiling, making encouraging sounds like 'Hmm, hmm,' or simply saying, 'Say a bit more,' all convey warmth and interest.

Accepting responses

Accepting responses convey our respect for others and help to create a trusting relationship. They show that we are not judging or criticizing. For example, a bereaved man says, 'I can't seem to concentrate at work any more'. An accepting response would be, 'It's hard when something so momentous has happened'. A non-accepting response would be, 'It's time you pulled yourself together!'

Reflection and empathy

By reflecting back to the client what we have heard, we can help people to continue to explore their needs. At the simplest level this involves repetition of what the client has said in a tentatively questioning tone. For example, a young wife says, 'I don't want my husband told this; I know he will give up'. You simply say, 'You think your husband will give up?' or 'Give up...?'

A more reflective way of responding is to paraphrase what the client says. This means restating what was said in your own words. It helps to use the phrases 'You seem to be saying...' or 'It sounds as if...'. A paraphrase of the above example would be, 'You seem to be saying that you would rather we did not speak to your husband about this because you feel that he may turn his face to the wall?' To give another example, a patient says, 'I'm still in pain and I don't know whose advice to take'. You could respond with the paraphrase, 'It sounds as if you feel that things are out of control at the moment and you don't know who to turn to'.

It would help the young wife in our earlier example to feel that we are really sensitive to her concerns if we convey that we have understood what she is feeling as well as what she is saying. We can do this by naming the feelings that are either directly expressed or conveyed in the tone of voice or body language. For example, we could say, 'It sounds as though you are frightened that if we talk to your husband about this, he may not want to go on living?' To give another example, the patient says to you, 'The doctor comes every day. I don't know why he needs to come so often because he doesn't talk to me about what's wrong. I think he talks to my wife, though. She goes out to the car with him and the last few times she's not come straight back up to me. I can hear her crying downstairs.' An empathic, reflective response would be, 'It sounds as if you are feeling anxious that the doctor is telling your wife things that you ought to know.'

Naming the feelings expresses empathy and helps people to feel that we really understand what is troubling them. It also gives them implicit permission to talk about their feelings. By responding gently and tentatively we show that we are not making assumptions but are prepared to learn more about their world. One way of ensuring that we are responding empathically is to use phrases such as, 'You feel ... because...,' or, 'It sounds as if you are feeling ... when...'. The exact words are not important, however: they merely provide a framework for communicating empathic understanding.

Repetition, paraphrasing and empathic responding all indicate that we are listening and trying to understand. By accurately reflecting the feelings behind the words we help people explore their responses further. We may also need to find out more about what the person is thinking and feeling and we can do this by asking questions.

Direct and indirect questions

There are two kinds of question. Direct questions demand a specific answer and are best used when factual answers are required, for example, 'Do you get the pain when you move?' or 'Have you taken your medication this morning?' Direct questions provide focus and close down the conversational options. They do not encourage people to divulge unrequested information. Indirect questions, on the other hand, give people a chance to answer in any way they choose. They invite people to tell us more. We could have asked the young wife in our example, 'What do you understand about your husband's illness?' 'Why' can be used but only with caution, as it can appear interrogative and probing. These questions are sometimes called open questions because they invite people to tell us more and 'open up' the conversation, for example:

- 'What is the worst thing?'
- 'When have you felt like this before?'
- 'How have you managed that before?'
- 'What is helping you most at this moment?'
- 'What else would help?'

Reviewing

It helps to review or summarize what has been heard, the feelings explored and actions that have been agreed. This is useful at the close of any dialogue, to clarify that both parties are in agreement. A summary of our previous example would be, 'We've been talking about your fears about your husband's reactions should he be told that his cancer has spread. He's been very depressed before and you are worried that he may withdraw from you and the children. Despite your anxieties you now feel that it would be okay for us to explore what he thinks is happening to him and you would like to be there when we speak to him. I'd like to talk to Dr Brown and get back to you later to arrange a time. How does that sound to you?'

It can also be useful to review what the other person is saying during the interaction, particularly when complex situations are being described or when the speaker is darting from one topic to another. Brief summaries slow the flow of information and help us check the assumptions that will be forming in our minds about the client's main concerns. An example from the above case would be, 'Let me just check that I'm understanding. Your husband has very gloomy periods and what is worrying you is that he may give up and withdraw from you and the family. At the same time you know he is worried about what's happening and you feel that keeping secret the information about his disease would also affect your relationship.'

Silence

Periods of silence are common when people are confronting painful feelings. It is important to let these happen, as they indicate that clients are reflecting on what they have said or are getting in touch with their feelings. Silences feel much longer to the listener than they do to the speaker and it can be tempting to rush in to fill the gap with a response. Our presence alone can help the client feel safe when confronting powerful feelings. Interrupting too soon can distract the client. It is important to carry on listening during silences, noting facial expressions and gestures. In this way we can sense when to break the silence. Silences that go on for too long can become very uncomfortable. A good way of breaking silence is to say tentatively, 'I'm wondering, what were you thinking just then?'

Touch

Sometimes there is nothing to say, or words feel inadequate, but touch, holding a hand or putting an arm around a shoulder, can convey support powerfully. We need to take care about the way we touch others, however, to ensure that we are conveying the message we intend. People respond in different ways and some hate being touched. Touching another person's back, hand or arm is more tentative, more neutral and less intimate than touching a knee or enveloping the other person in a hug. An experienced Macmillan nurse came to realize that she often touched people because she could not bear feeling helpless. She was trying to take away their emotional pain. Having realized that what she was doing was a reflection of her own needs, she came to use touch less frequently and more sensitively, as a way of conveying that she was sharing the pain.

Challenging

At times we may sense that other feelings are present behind the scene. This may be conveyed by incongruities between verbal and non-verbal behaviour, or by inconsistencies. A challenging response would be, 'Although you are describing very sad and difficult events, I notice that you are smiling.' Challenging responses may enable people to explore their feelings and responses at a deeper level. For example, 'You keep telling me that your husband did everything for you and now you can do nothing for yourself. However, my experience of you is that you are intelligent and able. Is it possible that you are not quite as helpless as you feel?'

Listening with the 'third ear'

Clients often have fears that they find difficult to voice. We should always be alert to hidden questions or fears. Empathy also involves listening to what is not being said and reflecting back to clients what we suspect they may be implying. This enables clients to explore deeper thoughts and feelings.

Rashid's wife was admitted to hospital with severe pain. He was much relieved when she became relatively symptom free but found himself feeling increasingly angry with her, especially after the social worker began to explore with him how he was going to manage at home now his wife's condition was rapidly deteriorating. The nurses reported that Rashid had been openly hostile to his wife and asked the social worker to explore this with him. During their conversation Rashid expressed his genuine relief that his wife was out of pain but also how angry he felt at having to cope with everything and how difficult it was for him to visit. She sensed that he was feeling guilty and said, 'You seem to be relieved that your wife is no longer in pain but you are also angry with her because you are having to cope with everything. I wonder if you feel guilty about this?' Rashid replied, 'That's exactly how I feel. I want to help her but I just make things worse. I don't know what comes over me. I don't want to burden her with all the problems at home. Before we always made decisions together and now we can't.' The social worker went on to suggest that as his wife was experiencing less pain she too might be feeling isolated and that they might still be able to make decisions together. Rashid decided to try to explain to his wife why he had been angry and how much he missed her.

Counselling skills checklist

In our experience what clients appreciate most is the feeling that we are really trying to understand. They will forgive us if we get it slightly wrong as long as we are demonstrating the core components of respect, genuineness and empathy. The way we attend and listen can enable people to trust us, open up, and allow us to enter their world. To help us check the quality of our interactions it is useful to ask ourselves the following questions.

- What am I conveying?
- Is the patient experiencing me as fully present?
- Does my non-verbal behaviour reinforce this?
- In what ways am I being distracted from giving my full attention? (Is there noise, time pressure, hunger, tiredness?)
- What can I do about any distractions?
- Am I using indirect questions?
- Am I checking my assumptions?
- How am I conveying my understanding?
- How am I reacting to what I am hearing?

Particular Issues for Counselling in Palliative Care
Confidentiality

It is easy to assume that everyone knows what is meant by maintaining confidentiality, but often people hold different views.

For example, the nursing team may decide that personal information concerning a family should not be divulged to other members of the wider team involved with the family. This area of potential conflict needs regular discussion both within multidisciplinary teams and between hospital, hospice and community-based teams.

It is dangerous to offer one-to-one confidentiality; not only may an individual become overwhelmed, but vital information may not be available when important decisions are being made. It is best to clarify that confidentiality will be honoured within the team. The nurse can explain this by saying something like, 'I don't need to share everything with my colleagues that you are telling me, or to write everything down, but there are some things that need to be shared with other members of the team who may be able to help you more than I can.' It is our experience that most patients and carers recognize the sense of this. However, respect for privacy and confidentiality should be striven for at all times and should be the subject of continuous appraisal. This respect should also be shown in what we write about people in files. Everyone has the right to see what has been written about them and it is not unusual for people to request to see their files.

Transference

The concept of transference is not generally taught to those involved in palliative care, since it is seen to be associated with psychiatric care. As a result it may go unrecognized.

The term 'transference' was coined by Freud to account for the tendency of certain patients to misperceive in (or transfer to) the therapist the characteristics of a parent or other significant person. This is not altogether surprising when we realize that the child's view of the world reflects that of the child's own family. Each person's family is 'normal' – it is, if you like, the norm to which every other family is compared. The child's view of 'fathers' reflects the behaviour of the particular father and of 'mothers' the mother. Later in life these perceptions are easily re-evoked at times when people are compellingly reminded of their childhood. This is particularly likely to occur when illness or bereavement undermines our confidence in our ability to cope and forces us to rely on others. In these circumstances a person who was repeatedly abused or betrayed by a parent may be found to distrust all in authority and to treat doctors and nurses with undue suspicion. It is hardly surprising if caring staff are upset and puzzled by such behaviour. It helps to remind ourselves that 'difficult' patients of this kind are often struggling to deal with feelings that belong to another relationship and another time.

We can achieve the aims of counselling in palliative care by:

- creating an environment in which it feels safe to express uncomfortable feelings such as anger, guilt and sadness;
- being non-judgemental and accepting of patients and those close to them;
- being honest about what we know, or do not know, about the progress of the disease and being prepared to find out;
- sharing our sadness that what is happening, or has happened, is awful, confusing and at times intolerable.

We can hinder by:

- indicating that we are too busy to respond;
- conveying that we are not prepared to go beyond the surface;
- feeling so helpless that we are not open to considering who else might help in a situation which is beyond us;
- being unprepared to experience feelings that the patient or the family want to share;
- being dishonest by pretending that we possess more knowledge than we have and not recognizing when we are out of our depth;
- minimizing the situation, for example, by rushing in to reassure instead of listening to the problems that the patient is struggling to express;
- not recognizing the impact on ourselves.

Conclusion

Developing confidence in using counselling skills enriches every point of contact: the physical care, the symptom control and the support offered to the bereaved family. We hope that this chapter will have helped you to feel more confident about what you do well while developing an awareness of where you may need to improve. A chapter on counselling cannot, however, take the place of a training course in which skills can be practised. There are now many courses available, ranging from short introductory inter-personal and counselling skills courses, to certificates and diplomas in counselling and bereavement counselling. Training provides an opportunity for reflection and to deepen awareness but most of all it allows us to practise skills in safety so that we can become more confident about this vital everyday aspect of our work.

Summary

❑   The aim of counselling is usually to help the other person to feel valued, respected and resourceful.

❑   Sharing the experience of illness helps patients and their caregivers come to terms with the impact of critical illness.

❑   Giving reassurance is seldom successful unless information is given at the same time.

❑   Counselling should be practised within a recognized code of ethics. It should: be focused, with specific goals; move towards the client's autonomy; be time limited; be a one-way relationship; involve explicit agreement that the client is working towards change; be supported by a programme of training; and be supervised.

❑   Three fundamental components of non-directive counselling are the capacity to respect others, accurately to perceive feelings that the other person is experiencing (empathy) and to be ourselves (genuineness).

❑   In order to be able to understand what other people are trying to tell us we must listen to all verbal and non-verbal aspects of communication, not just to the words.

❑   Distraction may be external or internal. Differences in value systems, race, culture, gender, education, use of vocabulary or class background can block our ability to hear what the other person is saying. It is important to develop awareness of our personal filters.

❑   We demonstrate our support and willingness to understand by listening, encouraging, accepting, reflecting, asking direct or indirect questions, reviewing, silence, touching, challenging, and listening with the third ear.

❑   Privacy and confidentiality within the team should be striven for at all times.

❑   Misperceptions of a counsellor often result from the transference of assumptions and feelings that properly belong to an earlier relationship, usually with parents.

❑   We can hinder by indicating that we are too busy to respond, not prepared to go beyond the surface, not open to considering who else might help, unprepared to risk sharing, dishonest, pretending that we possess more knowledge than we have, minimizing the situation or not recognizing the impact on ourselves.

4

Counselling the Patient with a Life-Threatening Illness

Doctors, nurses and other members of the caring team become very important people in the lives of seriously ill patients. Ideally we should provide continuity of care, although this is not always possible. General practitioners can often provide the continuity which the surgeon or radiotherapist cannot; for this reason they are of especial importance and should make it clear to the patient that they remain available and interested even after the patient has been referred to a 'specialist' for treatment.

In this chapter we consider how psychosocial care can be given to patients; in later chapters we focus on their families. We start by describing the course taken by most cancers and the influence that this has on the typical ways in which people with cancer respond to the illness. Uniformity is not to be expected and we describe two common ways of coping which have important implications for the counsellor at all stages of the illness: confrontation and avoidance. There are a number of steps in the progress of the disease. Help given at each stage helps to cement the trust between carer and patient and prepares the patient for the next stage. We outline the care that is needed when bad news is broken, the subsequent fears and griefs that emerge, and the ways in which members of the caring professions can be of help. We move on to consider the support that is needed when people are approaching death.

In order to focus this chapter we shall be writing mainly about people with cancer and it is cancer that most often comes to mind when people speak of 'terminal illness'. Yet cancer is not the commonest cause of death and there are many other illnesses whose prognosis is poor. We shall look more closely at some of these at the end of the chapter.

The Course of Cancer

It was Elizabeth Kübler-Ross's important studies of cancer patients that drew attention to the needs of this group of patients (Kübler-Ross, 1970). She described 'phases of dying', which led people to believe that both cancer and the way people respond to it follow a predictable pattern. Subsequent research showed that neither is as predictable as Kübler-Ross indicated. It is true that many people with cancer move, in time, from a state of relative unawareness of their situation to a greater degree of 'acceptance' and many of them show some of the reactions which Kübler-Ross calls 'phases', although not necessarily in the order in which she describes them. 'Denial', 'anger', 'bargaining', 'depression' and 'acceptance' may occur or they may not. Everything seems to depend on the person and the circumstances.

Cancer seldom follows a steady downhill course. More often it takes a series of steps and, even in those cases which have a bad prognosis from the start, the length of time between the steps is hard to predict. Typically a symptom will be the first sign that something is wrong; a lump appears or a pain is felt. Sometimes, as in the case of cancer of the breast, the patient is likely to be aware from the start that this is probably a cancer and that it may prove fatal. Other cancers, such as cancers of the stomach or pancreas, may be much more difficult to diagnose and may cause long periods of indeterminate illness before a diagnosis is reached. Some cancers are curable, some are incurable but follow a very long course, while others are rapidly fatal.

Most cancers can be treated and there are many that can be cured. Even when no cure has been possible there is likely to be a period of improvement before the condition recurs. If the disease has been detected early, the treatment may not be drastic: simple surgery, chemotherapy or radiotherapy in a dosage that does not leave the patient seriously damaged may be all that is needed. But if the patient suffers a recurrence the situation will usually demand drastic treatment. Most of the treatments for cancer damage healthy tissue as well as cancerous tissue. If the growth is extensive, either a wide excision is likely to be needed (with lasting mutilation as a result) or the patient must be subjected to poisoning with drugs or radiotherapy in the hope that the tumour cells will be more easy to kill than the healthy cells that surround them. Either way, patients are likely to feel very much worse before they feel better and they may be permanently damaged by the treatment.

Only when any reasonable hope of cure is gone will drastic treatment be discontinued. There are some doctors who never give up, and the consequences of this for the patient can be awful. Cancer is bad enough to put up with without the depredations of over-zealous doctors whose treatments may be worse than the disease they are attempting to cure. From the patient's point of view the cessation of treatment aimed at cure often removes a source of misery. It is usually possible to keep people free of pain and other distressing symptoms, although some patients, particularly those who have set great store by their strength or beauty, find it hard to accept weakness and (sometimes) emaciation. On the other hand, the loss of all appetites, including the appetite for life, can be regarded as one of the merciful aspects of cancer. It is much easier to slip quietly away if the urge to fight for life is gone, and this is not necessarily a time of great suffering. One patient compared it to the feeling of satisfaction that comes after a good meal. 'When you've had enough,' she said, 'You don't want a second helping.'

Reactions to Cancer

At each stage in the progression of the illness the patient is faced with a different set of problems. The first begins when the bad news of the diagnosis is broken. Initially the shock of becoming aware that you have a life-threatening illness may be considerable, and then fear is the predominant emotion. A period of insecurity is likely to follow, with the person having to live with uncertainty. Most are optimistic at this time and may continue on their accustomed paths without great disruption. But a recurrence brings in its train not only more bad news about the future but also very real physical and functional losses, which are a real cause of grief. People grieve for their inability to work, to play, to have sex or whatever other losses may result from their illness. Afterwards there may follow another relatively calm plateau until the next setback.

Viewed in this way the course of cancer is likely to be stepwise, with each step triggered by a setback and the impact of bad news followed by a period of grieving as the patient comes to terms with the new situation. The world has become a very frightening place in which terrible things can happen. The more a person has suffered, the more dread there is of further suffering. If a little illness is bad, it is logical for the patient to expect that, as the disease progresses, the symptoms will get worse. It may come as a considerable surprise, therefore, if the later stages are less painful and unpleasant than those that preceded them, yet this is often the case. Perhaps because of this, some people achieve a peace of mind in the later stages of cancer which contrasts with the fear and distress of the earlier period.

Styles of Coping

How people cope with these problems is a very personal thing. At the risk of over-simplifying the complexity of human personality, it is worth classifying people in two different ways: as *thinkers* versus *feelers*, and as *confronters* versus *avoiders*. Most of us lie somewhere between these extremes, but it is useful to consider them as if they were separate, since the extent to which people approach one or other extreme will influence, in important ways, the types of problem they face and the ways in which we can help them.

Thinkers and feelers

In general there are two ways of getting things done: one is to do it yourself, and the other is to find someone else to do it for you. Both are appropriate in certain circumstances, but, regardless of this, there are some people who favour one method of coping rather than the other. In families and cultures in which 'self-reliance' is a virtue and 'independence' the predominant value, people are encouraged to 'stand on their own two feet' and not to 'be a burden to others'. In order to do this such people tend to value thinking (which aids self-control) over feeling (which attracts nurturance and support). On the other hand, there are some families and cultures in which passivity, obedience to authority, fitting in and not 'rocking the boat' by asserting oneself encourage rather the virtues of co-operation, humility and respect. They tend towards the feeling rather than the thinking end of the spectrum.

People brought up in the former type of culture tend to think of themselves as being in control of their own destiny (in psychologists' jargon they have a 'high internal locus of control'), whereas people brought up in the latter feel as if their lives are controlled by others (their 'locus of control' is 'external').

These attitudes of mind encourage very different methods of coping with problems. Those who see themselves as being, or needing to be, in control, tend to be assertive, masterful and active. Those who see others as being in control tend to be passive, affectionate and perhaps seductive, since these are the best ways of persuading others to control things on their behalf. The former run into difficulties when they can no longer succeed in remaining independent of others, the latter when there is nobody on whom they can rely. Illness, by reducing a person's ability to remain independent, often creates situations in which people can no longer 'stand on their own two feet'. It may also cause the more passive to make demands on others which the others are not able or willing to meet. In either case problems are likely to arise.

Thinkers try to find solutions to all problems. They are often very controlled people who keep their feelings to themselves and seldom ask for help; they are action men and women, who find it hard to do nothing. Feelers take a more passive attitude. They cry easily and do not hesitate to lean on others when the need arises. They are warmer and more affectionate than thinkers but less able to make plans and stick to them. Faced with a serious illness, thinkers try to make plans and to find some way of controlling events. As long as their plans are effective they cope well, but they find it difficult to accept that there are some things that they cannot control. Rather than admit their own inability they will blame their symptoms on the treatments they are receiving, distrust their medical attendants and question every decision that we try to make on their behalf. Consequently they are often 'difficult patients'.

On the other hand, feelers wear their hearts on their sleeves. They may have very little confidence in their ability to control the world but are quite happy to let others do it for them. When they are faced with a serious illness they sometimes cling to doctors or nurses, who are seen as all powerful. They are grateful for everything we do for them and prefer not to be asked to make their own decisions. They often cry a great deal and make us feel guilty because we know we are not the miracle workers they want us to be.

Feelers are in touch with their feelings; we know where we stand with them. Their problems lie in the direction of taking initiatives and replanning their lives rather than expressing grief and showing feelings. By contrast thinkers bottle up their feelings and may need to be encouraged to share them. They may also need reassurance that we shall not lose respect for them if they do.

Cultural factors often decide whether a person will become a thinker or a feeler. In current northern European society children are taught to keep a 'stiff upper lip' in the face of adversity, whereas in southern Europe they learn that it is all right to respond emotionally to situations. Similarly there are differences within cultures regarding the freedom with which men and women are permitted to express feelings. On the whole, northern European culture encourages men to be thinkers and women feelers, although there are many exceptions.

There are both advantages and disadvantages to the inhibition and expression of feelings: inhibition helps us to deal calmly with emergencies, while expression signals to others just how we are feeling. Partnerships in which one person is good at thinking and the other at feeling may achieve a balance between the two.

Occupations also play a part in determining how people react and respond. Soldiers are under strong cultural pressure to control their feelings. Similarly police officers and surgeons need to exert strict control of their emotions in order to cope with the more horrifying aspects of their jobs. It may well be that these occupations tend to attract people who are already well in control and their training then increases this capacity.

On the other hand, those professions in which tenderness and the sharing of emotion are desirable, such as social work, psychiatry and counselling, tend to attract people who are in touch with their feelings and to encourage them in their training programmes.

To some extent people can adapt to circumstances. Thus some may be tough at work and tender at home. But this is the exception rather than the rule, and many of the problems which are met in counselling stem from the difficulties which people have when faced with a situation in which their customary way of coping no longer enables them to cope effectively.

Confrontation and avoidance

Although we tend to assume that thinkers confront problems and feelers avoid them this is not necessarily the case. Thinkers often avoid situations that will arouse feelings and feelers may be better than thinkers at confronting social situations in which gentleness, tact and empathy are more useful than cold reason.

The tendency to confront problems rather than to avoid them stems essentially from confidence in ourselves and others. This, as we saw in Chapter 1, is a reflection of our sense of security and may itself reflect previous experiences of life, perhaps in childhood.

Both confrontation and avoidance may be appropriate in certain circumstances. If we are inundated with so many problems that we cannot possibly cope with them all at once, we must put some aside in order to give our full attention to others. This is obvious in emergencies, when it may be necessary to put our feelings on 'hold' for a while in order to keep calm enough to make vital decisions. Less obvious is the handling of long-term dangers which are not going to go away and about which we can do very little. People with cancer have to learn to live with the dangers and uncertainties of their life. They cannot spend all their time feeling fear or thinking about cancer. They have to get on with the ordinary business of living – planning the next meal, getting the children to school, and so on. They can do this only if they find some way of avoiding the thoughts and feelings which are constantly threatening to well up inside them. It is not surprising that many people with cancer pretend that their illness is not as serious as it is, avoid talking about the facts of the illness and interpret any change in their symptoms in an optimistic way. To dismiss this type of behaviour as 'denial' is to misunderstand it.

Problems of avoidance and obsessional confrontation

Avoidance can become a problem if:

- people continually avoid facing up to their problems and making necessary plans (for example by refusing to go to the doctor when a new symptom emerges),
- their attempts at avoidance are so rigorous that they lead to a build up of unexpressed emotion which then emerges in distorted forms (such as psychosomatic or hypochondriacal illness), or
- the effort required to maintain the avoidance interferes with other psychological functioning (for example by causing insomnia, stultifying spontaneous emotional expression or causing people to act in an excessively guarded or defensive way).

These difficulties will not emerge if people with cancer opt to spend a reasonable amount of time thinking about the implications of their illness and expressing their feelings about it. There is, however, a limit to what is reasonable and some patients become obsessed and preoccupied with morbid thoughts about the illness. Their waking hours are filled with repetitive agonizing, which may then continue in their dreams. They find it difficult to cope with responsibilities that they would ordinarily take in their stride and may, in consequence, retreat from the world. They become withdrawn and isolated from the people and situations which would normally distract them from continuous grieving.

This is the other side of the coin of avoidance. If avoidant patients are unable to tackle problems for fear that they will lose control, obsessively preoccupied patients are unable to switch off the thoughts that occupy their minds. The crucial issue in both cases is *control*. Both types of patient will be helped if they begin to believe that they are in control of their own thoughts and feelings, that they can switch them on and off at will, and that nothing dreadful will happen if they do either of these things.

Most people's ways of coping lie within the extremes of the types of thinking and feeling, and confronting and avoiding. However, we usually tend towards one extreme rather than the other and it can be helpful for caregivers to identify where the patient lies along these continua in order to respond with understanding to the problems that arise. To some extent we can influence the situation and reactions.

Peter always kept his feelings to himself. When doctors or nurses asked how he was, he regularly replied, 'Fine, fine'. On one occasion, when his symptoms were worse and his family had failed to visit, a nurse ignored his bravado and sat with him on the bed holding his hand. Her whole posture suggested that, however brave Peter was being, they both knew that things were anything but 'fine'. No words passed between them but a tear crept down Peter's face and, after a few minutes, he said, 'Thank you, nurse, I needed that.'

The implications of these coping styles will become clear as we trace the patient's history through the course of the illness. We start at the point where the doctor has become aware of the patient's diagnosis and prognosis. The doctor is then faced with a dilemma: what should the patient be told?

Breaking Bad News

Information is essential if we are to cope realistically with life and death, yet the communication of information about cancer often fails. Sometimes this is because the patient is adopting an avoidant style of coping, but very often it is not the patient but doctors or family members who obstruct the flow. A doctor may fail to give information or deliberately mislead patients for fear that the truth will somehow destroy them. Family members may collude or put pressure on the doctor to do this out of a similar wish to protect patients from suffering. The idea that 'ignorance is bliss' may lead to concealment of the facts of the diagnosis or prognosis in ways, which, however well intentioned, deprive patients of any chance of making good use of the life that remains to them. We all have a right to know the truth about things that affect our lives.

From the patient's point of view this can be very confusing. Most patients are clever enough to notice when doctors give inconsistent answers or do not invite questions. Time and again one of us (CMP) has been told, 'You know, you're the first doctor to invite questions.' Clearly if the patient has noticed that, with this kind of illness, doctors are afraid to invite questions, he or she will have deduced that whatever it is that is wrong is very frightening indeed. Far from reassuring the patient, the doctor's silence has become a source of fear. Similarly the doctor who lies seldom takes the trouble to ensure that all the team tell the same lie, and sooner or later patients realize that the answers they are getting are inconsistent and that somebody is lying. Once a doctor has been caught out in a lie all basis for trust in the relationship has been lost. The patient may then disbelieve *all* doctors.

Sometimes it is the patient who misunderstands or fails to hear the information that has been given. This is likely to occur if patients are very anxious or if they are given more information than they can take. Alternatively the doctor may have used words which the patient does not understand. Even common words like 'cancer' and 'death' mean different things to different people.

Nobody can take in more than one thing at a time and people who are anxious or fearful often find it more than usually difficult to take in what they are told. Information of enormous import will, therefore, take time to digest. It follows that it takes time to break bad news.

Breaking bad news is like major surgery. Whether we like it or not we are inflicting a psychological injury which is every bit as damaging as the amputation of a limb. Like an amputation it requires time, planning and a proper place to carry out the operation. Giving neutral information is easy and takes little time, but when breaking bad news we need to be aware of the impact of what we are saying. If we are to demonstrate our willingness to understand, then we must set aside sufficient time and plan the session so that we are giving 'bite-sized' pieces of information and enabling people to respond.

It is easier to give and receive information if the environment feels safe. We should, therefore, choose a private and comfortable place where we shall not be interrupted. The best place to break bad news is usually the patient's home; this is where people feel safest and where they are most likely to have family and friends to support them. More commonly we have to break bad news in a hospital or hospice. We should at least try to choose a room that is home-like. Sadly the architects of modern hospitals seem more intent on providing the physical facilities for care than the psychological. Time and again we are forced to attempt to communicate with patients and families in an inhospitable room geared to treatment or examination and filled with the glittering instruments and gruesome posters of the age of technology.

Many patients prefer their spouse or partner to be present at such times, but there are others who prefer to meet the doctor alone or with some other member of the family, perhaps because their spouse is very anxious. It is best to let the patient decide who, if anyone, should come, but to take note that others may need separate help if they have been omitted.

Even if we already know the patient, it is worth spending a little time introducing ourselves and establishing an atmosphere of friendly support. A smile, a shake of the hand and a few casual remarks will relieve tension and pave the way to more serious matters. Before imparting information it is a good idea to find out what the other person already knows or thinks he or she knows. A question such as 'What have the doctors told you about this illness?' or 'Have you guessed what the problem is?' will often reveal that patients are already fully aware of the seriousness of the situation and have reached their own conclusions. This makes our task much easier, since all we have to do is to confirm what they already know or suspect and make sure that the words they use mean the same thing to us as they do to them. 'Yes, it is a kind of cancer, but there are many types of cancer. What does cancer mean to you?'

When there is a big gap to be bridged, it will take time to cross it and we may need to come back several times to answer further questions. Rather than assuming that we know best what patients need to know, it is better to let them decide their own priorities. The best way to do this is to invite questions. *People will seldom ask a question unless they are ready to hear the answer* and we should listen very carefully to the question before answering. There is a world of difference between the direct question, 'Is it cancer, doctor?', and the elliptical, 'Don't tell me it's cancer.' To the former a direct answer is indicated; in the latter case it is better to spend time finding out why the patient does not want to be told. 'Have you known anyone with cancer?' This question often elicits the family horror story, which may bear little relationship to the illness from which this patient is suffering.

Many of the fears of people with cancer are quite needless, but we will not find out about them unless we give the patient time to get round to them. It takes courage to ask, 'Will it be painful?', for the answer might be 'Yes'. We need to use our intuition and to be aware of the unasked questions. To many patients cancer means death in agony and it may come as a great surprise and relief to learn that this is not the case. In fact, whenever we talk about cancer it is wise to dispel some of the myths about it. Most cancers are not inherited, and nor are they caused by the patient's misdeeds. They cannot be caught by other members of the family and they do not inevitably lead to mutilation and severe, un-relieved pain.

Bad News and Coping Styles

Thinkers often give the impression that they can handle bad news very well. They remain calm, ask all the right questions and seem to be taking in the answers we give them. At times their matter-of-fact approach can be quite disconcerting. In such cases it is useful to ask them about their feelings. 'How do you feel about that?' may sound like an odd question, but it does imply that the patient is allowed to have feelings and to share them. Similarly it is often a good idea to reach out and touch someone if we sense that they are behaving a little too well. This then implies, 'I know you are being a hero, but you don't have to pretend to me. You are a human being and, like all human beings, need comfort when you hear frighten-ing things.' Non-verbal communication can convey this much more eloquently than words.

Feelers may become so upset that they are unable to continue to take in information at all. In these cases we may need to allow them more time for the information to sink in, but we should beware of being sucked into an over-protective role. It is not our sympathy but our calmness which the patient needs. Such patients need little encouragement to express their grief, but they may need help in figuring out the implications of the prognosis and making plans. Attempts to distract people from obsessive preoccupation are doomed to failure and may aggravate the problem by increasing their anxiety.

It is quite appropriate for people to confront their problems when bad news is being broken. It is only later, when the confronter will not leave things alone, that problems arise. Such patients persuade their doctors to tell them too much, too soon. Their anxious, obsessional determination to think of everything that might go wrong and to cross every bridge before they get to it can be exhausting to all concerned. Despite all that we have said about the right to information, there are times when we may serve patients best by refusing to be drawn into discussion of yet another 'What if...?' question and reassuring them that they can leave tomorrow's problems until tomorrow.

Perhaps the most difficult people to help are the avoiders. They seldom ask questions and may even say that they do not want to be told about their illness. They often fail to keep appointments when bad news is expected. If the doctor insists on telling them things they do not want to hear, they sometimes refuse to believe what they are told or rush out of the room. They may go from one unorthodox healer to another until they find someone who tells them what they want to hear. Some have a touching faith that a miracle will happen and remain convinced of this to the point of death. Others show by their behaviour that they are aware of the true situation, although they still refuse to discuss it.

To those who were trained to think of the repression or avoidance of problems as the main cause of psychiatric illness, the behaviour of the avoider is intolerable. However, this may be an effective coping strategy. People have a right to know the facts of their illness, but they also have a right to remain ignorant, and we should respect that right. Certainly we have no right to force information on people who make it clear that they do not want to be told. Having said this, we often find patients who start by avoiding the things that they fear and change their minds once they begin to feel safe. It may be a long time before they trust us enough to talk about the things they most fear, but if we wait patiently and indicate our willingness to go as far as they wish, but no further, they may surprise us. We should certainly not assume that someone who has avoided an issue on one occasion is always going to adopt this defence. If people seek our help with these problems this is an indication that they want to change, and we can reasonably play a more active role. Even so, we should be only one step ahead of them, not two.

Involving Others

Thus far we have spoken of communication as if this always takes place in isolation and nobody else is involved, but this is seldom the case. Others may be present: family members, fellow patients or staff. Each will be affected in their own way by the communication, and we need to be aware both of the part which they can play in caring and of their own needs for care and information. What is right for one member of a family may not be right for another, and we may have to choose carefully whom to include when communicating important information. The whole situation can become very complicated and we may need to involve every member of the caring team if we are to achieve very much. Even one-to-one communication takes place in the setting of a ward or home and it is valuable to recognize and involve others in the process whenever possible. In many hospices, notes recording significant communications with a patient or family member are recorded in a separate section of the case notes; these may be in a special colour to facilitate identification. This makes it easy for staff to find out what is going on and to play their own part in the ongoing process of communication. It also acts as a constant reminder of the importance of communication. Patients will sometimes choose the most unexpected moment to ask a crucial question or reveal an insight that had not previously been recognized. The recording of key communication issues on a specific sheet helps to ensure that these insights and opportunities will not be lost.

Ongoing Care

Once a diagnosis of life-threatening illness has been made, it is most important to ensure that every patient has the ongoing support of at least one and preferably more than one professional caregiver as long as he or she remains in danger. For the patient with cancer this means throughout the course of the illness. In the

National Health Service in Britain this is usually the GP, yet even in this setting continuity of care is often lost. The patient is referred to a 'specialist' and disappears from the sight and mind of the caregiver. To some extent membership of an organization for cancer patients (such as Cancerlink in the UK) can provide reassurance that information and support can be obtained quickly and easily when it is needed, but this is no substitute for individual care from a team who know enough about the patient's illness to speak with authority. Information centres are now being introduced in hospitals, to provide information on orthodox and complementary treatments, support and counselling. National organizations (such as BACUP in the UK) provide excellent information leaflets, telephone advice and counselling.

Once bad news has been received the two emotional problems for which help is likely to be needed are fear and grief.

Coping with fear

We all know that disasters happen, but most of the time they happen to other people – not to us. People who know they have cancer lose their sense of security, of being protected from danger. For a long time after the diagnosis has been made they are waiting for the next disaster to strike. Each little ache or pain is the cancer returning; appetite and weight are closely watched and any fluctuation may be taken to be a sign of deterioration; minor irregularities in subcutaneous fat are evidence of underlying growths; there is danger everywhere. Fear, as we have seen, causes its own symptoms, and it is all too easy for these symptoms to be misinterpreted as signs of cancer. Palpitations, digestive disturbances and the myriad aches and pains which can result from muscle tension and hyperalertness are all causes for alarm. The alarm generates more fear, and the fear more symptoms.

Contrary to expectation, *most of the pains experienced by cancer patients are not caused by cancer*. They are the minor pains caused by the stresses and strains of everyday life, tension headaches, back strain, and aches in any muscle or joint in the body. It has been said that most people suffer pain somewhere in their body every day and major pain is felt about once a week. The only difference is that, whereas the healthy person takes little notice of the ache, taking whatever action is needed to remove it by resting an aching muscle, relieving pressure on a joint by a change of posture or taking a brief period of exercise, people with cancer anxiously focus their attention upon the ache and worry it into a pain. Such worry causes the pain to get worse, as does any sensation that is magnified by fear.

This does not mean that such pains should be ignored or belittled. Medical and nursing staff who are in a position to reassure the patient about such minor symptoms have an important role to play. We need to be easily accessible to the patient and to respond rapidly and effectively to their requests for help. Not all patients will ask for help. Some keep their fears to themselves in the false belief that, because they have a fatal illness, nothing can be done for them.

All people who have had a cancer and who remain at risk of recurrence need regular outpatient appointments to ensure that problems of this kind are picked up and dealt with. The appointments themselves become occasions for anxious dread, but once they are over and the patient has had another 'dose' of reassurance, the patient can breathe more easily and the level of anxiety drops sharply. If, in addition, patients are told that they can contact their doctor 'at any time' if they have any problems, they will be reassured and may be less anxious, and less likely to develop and need help for anxiety-related symptoms.

But what of the patient whose illness is recurring? What if the pain *is* caused by cancer? Here the need for emotional support is greater than ever. All pain is aggravated by fear and it is important for the physician to treat the fear as well as the pain. If there is still a reasonable hope of cure the patient will usually accept the most drastic of treatments, but we should beware of taking advantage of the patient's fears to obtain acceptance of treatments that are only going to spoil the last phase of the patient's life. The wise physician knows when to stop active treatment and to move into the phase of palliative care.

Palliative care

The period from the end of active treatment until the patient's death varies in duration. Some patients will survive for many months; others may still be under active treatment at the time of their death. The advantages of a period of palliative care are that it allows time for the carers to achieve a good level of symptom control and the patient and family to prepare themselves for the patient's death. It is not appropriate here to discuss symptom control. However, great advances have been made in recent years and the reader is referred to Doyle *et al.* (1993) and to Twycross (1994) for authoritative accounts of this field.

This is a time when anxiety management, as outlined on pages 173–175, is often important, and every effort should be made to ensure that patients have the time and opportunity to share their fears and griefs. This will enable them to begin to confront the prospect of their own death. We tend to assume that the patient's greatest fear is of death itself, but most people are more afraid of dying than they are of being dead. It is a relief for them to learn that, for most patients, by the time they require terminal care the worst is already over.

Anna was a Greek Cypriot woman aged 43 with a carcinoma of the breast who was receiving palliative care in a general hospital. I (CMP) was asked by the nurses on her ward to see her in my capacity as liaison psychiatrist. She had been complaining of pain to the night nurses yet they did not think she was in pain and wanted to know if her pain was psychological in origin. Pain, of course, is very subjective: the only person who knows whether or not they are in pain is the patient and I tend to be sceptical when staff tell me that a pain is not 'real'. For this reason I asked a nurse to accompany me when I went to see the patient, as I thought it likely that she would need to feed back to other members of the team the outcome of our assessment. The nurse informed me that Anna had not been told her diagnosis or prognosis.

Having introduced myself to Anna, I explained the reason why I had been called and asked her what it was she had wanted from the night nurse. Rather to my surprise she answered, 'A cup of tea.' I had never heard of tea being used as a treatment for pain before so I asked her to explain further. She said that she knew that if she did this, the night nurse would sit with her while she drank it and they could talk. I said, 'That sounds like a good idea; what did you want to talk about?' Anna replied, 'Well, I've got cancer haven't I?' I replied, 'You've got a kind of cancer, but what does cancer mean to you?' She then told me that she had known a woman in Cyprus with cancer and 'Her eyes dropped out!' Now, I have never known anyone with cancer whose eyes dropped out and it was not difficult to reassure Anna that she had not got that kind of a cancer. I then asked, 'Is there anything else that's been worrying you?' She then told me about another patient who had had 'terrible, terrible pain'. I asked her if she was in pain and, rather to my surprise, she said 'No'.

It is not always easy to reassure people about pain. They do not necessarily believe a doctor's reassurance and it was necessary to give Anna a telephone number which she could ring if she ever had bad pain before she looked convinced. Her next remark was interesting. She said, 'I'm not frightened of dying,' and went on to tell me of her faith in God and of her certainty of a life hereafter. But she agreed that she had been frightened of the approach to death.

She was in good spirits when I left. I subsequently met her again and talked with her family, who, once they realized that she did not have long to live, seldom left her bedside. She died peacefully a few weeks later. There had been no more complaints of pain.

I never did find out the nature of Anna's 'pain'. Perhaps she was pretending to have pain in order to get the attention she needed or perhaps she was using the word 'pain' to mean 'mental pain', as they do in Greece, where *poenia* can be physical or mental. It was important for the nurses to understand that she knew a great deal more about her diagnosis and prognosis than they had imagined and for them to continue the reassurance that I had given.

The patient's grief

Grief may be expressed as anger, self-reproach, with guilt and loss of self-esteem, pining, or depression. Any or all of these may be experienced by people who are coming to the end of their lives.

Anger. Not everyone has Anna's faith and there are certainly some people who need to express their grief about the prospect of their own death. Anger is a common reaction to losses of all kinds and some blame God for their predicament. 'If there were a good God,' they say, 'He wouldn't allow this to happen.' Whatever one's personal faith, it is unwise to argue about this. Rather we need to accept that anger is a part of grieving and to show that we understand the patient's anger and despair. 'It is hard to believe that God is good when you have gone through all that you and your family have faced in the last year. It sounds as though you are angry with God.' Like tears, anger is better out than in, and we need to be prepared to let the wave of anger break over us. Only if we share the same religious background as the patient is it acceptable to give our own views, and then only if asked. We should avoid any temptation to take advantage of the patient's weakness to obtain a death-bed conversion. Chaplains and other clergy usually understand well the crises of faith that can arise at times such as this and will be of great value to those who want pastoral guidance.

Some people attempt to compensate for feelings of helplessness by becoming assertive and attempting to control us. This is usually seen as 'bad behaviour', but if we can see it as a kind of heroism in the face of overwhelming odds, we may be more likely to get on the right 'wavelength' and to help patients to regain their damaged self-esteem.

Kevin had always been combative. He was born in Ireland but had rejected Catholicism at an early age and was well known in the factory where he worked as a shop steward who could get the entire workforce out on strike. He found the nurses on his ward at the hospice 'Too bloody nice' and in no time had insulted the chaplain and doctors. The only person who could get on with him at all was an Irish nun who told him to 'Stop your nonsense'. With her he had a series of mutually enjoyable shouting matches. Whereas most patients would have been devastated by a member of staff who insulted them, Kevin liked nothing better. Throughout his life his self-esteem had rested on his ability to fight back against the odds and the nun had rightly guessed that he would enjoy a fight. When he died he left her his collection of gramophone records.

Guilt and loss of self-esteem. Anger and guilt often go together. People blame themselves for taking their anger out on those around them, they blame themselves for their illness, they feel guilty at being dependent on others and see themselves as a burden. Doctors and nurses can easily add to these feelings of self-reproach if we mistake the illness for the person who is ill. For instance, deafness, blindness and speech defects affect the carers almost as much as they affect the cared for. We too experience frustration if the patient is unable to communicate with us, and we may be tempted to express that irritation towards the patient. Similarly, people who are suffering from brain damage should not be blamed if they behave in ways that seem 'silly'. In all these circumstances we need to remind ourselves that both we and the patient are suffering from the illness – it is not the patient who is frustrating us.

Self-esteem is often built on certain attributes of which a person can feel proud. Achievements, secure attachments and the recognition of our worth by others all contribute to this. We can tolerate being inferior in one direction if we can make it up in another. People who have never attained much at school may compensate for this by building up physical strength. Others obtain credit by being beautiful, or friendly or generous to others. Quite small things sometimes have important consequences. Some people may pride themselves on their appearance or their expressive hands, others may be proud of their productivity (they may be good cooks or skilled at carpentry), and yet others will derive their self-esteem from their social skills, their ability to amuse or to get on with children.

Illness can take away many of the things which support self-esteem. When this happens, we not only grieve for what we have lost, but we lose our self-respect as well. It is extremely important for those who are caring for the sick to show that we understand that many skills have been diminished by illness and that, nevertheless, we continue to respect and value the sufferer regardless of these losses. Sadly, there are all too many professional carers who take advantage of the patient's weakness to bolster their own strength. We talk down to patients, treat them like children, ignore them, or act as if we owned them and the hospitals we work in. To some extent this is built into the system; we are the experts and we want the patient to do what we tell them. We do not want them to question our judgement or refuse our treatments. One of the rewards of the job is the adulation we receive and we soon get into the habit of thinking of ourselves as more important than the patient.

Some patients collude with this. They want to believe that we have magical powers and that our strength and wisdom will be used on their behalf. We shall only disappoint them if we insist on asking their opinions about everything. But that does not mean that we should not recognize the dangers inherent in the situation. The moment we express irritation or pity, the moment we treat the patient like a thing rather than a person, the moment we fail to respect the patient's rights, we are undermining that person and reducing the chance that he or she will find the courage to face up to the challenge of the illness.

Jill had always enjoyed baking but her mastectomy had caused lymphoedema of her right arm and she could no longer get her 'hands into the dough' as she had loved to do. The occupational therapist asked her if she would help one of the volunteers to bake cakes for the ward. Jill agreed and told the volunteer exactly what to do, testing the consistency of the mixture from time to time with her better hand. This became a regular partnership and a source of pride to both participants. It also gave pleasure to the staff and patients, who benefited from their labours.

Pining. This is the most characteristic feature of grief, and people who are coming near the end of their lives may pine for the jobs they have left, the home to which they will never return and the life they will never live. Sharing these griefs does help and the remarkable thing is that many patients do come through this grief relatively quickly, much quicker than their family. Perhaps this is because they do not have to start all over again: all they have to do is to let go, and the debility produced by the disease may make that easy.

Depression. This is not uncommon and may be severe. Some patients turn their faces to the wall and give up. They may even will themselves to die or ask for euthanasia when there is no good reason for them to do so. This is a very different reaction from 'acceptance' and reflects deep despair, helplessness and hopelessness. It is most likely to occur in people who have little trust in themselves or in others; they will often have had previous depressive episodes in the face of loss. The pattern of apathy, slowing of thoughts and movement, and general negativism such that nothing we suggest seems to help, is difficult to tackle by counselling alone. The patient may be just too depressed to let us near and too slowed down to get thoughts together in any useful way. Fortunately this type of depression responds very well to antidepressant medication.

The risk of suicide

Occasionally patients are so depressed that they commit suicide. The surprising thing is that, with all the public debates on euthanasia, suicide is still very rare among cancer patients. The commonest means to suicide is an overdose of antidepressant medication and doctors need to be very cautious when prescribing these drugs for potentially suicidal patients. Fortunately, the newer antidepressants, such as fluoxetine, are relatively safe.

All caregivers should assess the risk of suicide whenever they meet a patient who is unusually depressed or agitated. The simple way to do this is to ask, 'Has it been so bad you have wanted to kill yourself?' This question will nearly always elicit an honest answer. We will not have put the idea into the patient's head – people who are *that* depressed have always thought of it already. Suicidal patients will have worked out a plan and will be able to tell us how they intend to kill themselves. Threats of this kind should always be taken seriously. Where possible we should remove the means to suicide but should be aware that, in doing so, we are removing a means of escape. In such cases we need to offer the patient an alternative. The patient at home may be given the telephone number of a person whom they can call at any time of the day or night if they become desperate, this may be the number of a hospice home care team, a GP or the Samaritans.

Whenever we suspect that there is a risk of suicide we should discuss our management of the case with a senior colleague. Usually we should also discuss the situation with the patient's GP and family. Such precautions usually result in everyone rallying round in support and the risk may soon pass. Occasionally a psychiatric referral is indicated.

Within a hospital or hospice it is easier to provide people with the supervision and support which will make it most unlikely that they will commit suicide. The most difficult to predict is the impulsive act of a person whose mood is fluctuating. This is most likely to occur in patients who are getting confused and disorientated. An open window or balcony is a constant invitation to such people, who should be kept away from such temptation.

The Approach to Death

Most patients lose consciousness well before the moment of death. For them their last experience of life is a quiet slipping away which is a far cry from the dramatic image of death conveyed by the mass media. Volunteer helpers may be able to sit with patients who are close to death if the staff are too busy and no family or friends are available. Many patients are afraid that they will die alone and we should do everything in our power to ensure that they do not. The patient who is left alone behind drawn curtains is an advertisement to all on the ward that we do not care. Even a deeply unconscious patient should not be left alone. We may think that they are unaware of what is going on around them but other patients are watching and are always upset if an unconscious person is treated as if already dead. Patients who have been unconscious often regain consciousness and staff have sometimes been embarrassed to discover that an 'unconscious' patient was fully aware of what was going on even though he or she could not move or otherwise respond. It follows that those who are at the bedside of a dying patient should continue to act as if he or she were present and able to hear everything that is going on. If the family are not present it is important for a member of staff to stay close.

There can be no more awesome moment than the moment of death. We owe it to ourselves as well as to the patient and family to give it the solemnity it deserves. For caring staff as well as for family members this is a time when we must put all other priorities and considerations on 'hold'. We may be worked off our feet, harassed by impatient patients and importunate families, but a staff member *must* find the time to be with the patient and family at this moment. This may not be easy. The patient may be unconscious, the family tired out. There may be nothing practical that can be done, and none of us knows the precise moment when death will come. It is tempting to send the family away: 'There's nothing more you can do,' we say, and we think there is nothing more that *we* can do.

For the families of patients who are dying at home, the knowledge that a nurse is accessible by telephone to give advice and is willing to come out if the patient is dying can be a great reassurance.

The Dying Child

It is not possible to discuss here the many different ways in which terminal illness can affect the lives of children of various ages. The interested person is advised to read Blueblond-Langner (1978) and Hindmarsh (1993). All that we can do here is to draw out a few general points for consideration.

When it is a child who is dying there is a tendency for parents and staff to collude to conceal from the child the seriousness of the situation. This is a very understandable reaction: nobody wants to burden a child with the terrifying prospect of death and we like to pretend that children know nothing about this awesome topic. But a little reflection gives us pause. Children think a great deal about death; many children's games are death games and from an early age they are playing at death. When children are ill they easily read the message in the eyes of people around them and group work with youngsters with cancer shows that they regularly know more about their illness than their parents imagine.

Just as adult patients often get the message that, with this kind of illness, doctors do not invite questions, so children get the message that they had better not talk to the adults about what is happening to them. Some are very frightened by this isolation from the people they rely on to give them support.

The important implication of this observation is not that we should force every child to face the prospect of death, but that we should try to find out what children are thinking so that we can help them in the way that is right for them. This will sometimes mean that we shall find ourselves talking about the fact that they have noticed that this illness is getting worse, that other children have died from it and that they may die too. Like adults, they may need to grieve for the people and things they are losing in the course of coming to terms with the life they still have to lead. Children are practical creatures who find it easier than adults to live in the present. They need to be kept free of pain and other distressing symptoms and they need the love and care of their family. Given these two things, there is no reason why the death of a child should not be peaceful.

Of course, the parents are the people who are best placed to know what is going on in the minds of their children and we should not attempt to displace or rival them. Any support we give to children should be given with the full collaboration and consent of the parents. Much of the support given by counsellors to children is indirect; by helping the parents we help them to help the children. We shall return to this in the next chapter.

Counselling Patients with Other Types of Illness

Apart from cancer, the illnesses which are most likely to be seen as 'terminal' are AIDS, motor neurone disease and certain other neurological conditions. These are all rare causes of death and, before we go on to consider them, it is worth asking why the commoner causes of death, such as myocardial infarction and strokes, are seldom seen as 'terminal'. The answer, of course, is that many people who have these diseases do recover from them. This makes it very difficult to persuade professional carers to consider the possibility that they will prove fatal. We like to be optimistic and see no reason to help people to prepare themselves for something that may never happen. There would be no harm in this if the patients themselves always shared this view. But there are many patients who, after their second coronary attack or after living with chronic heart failure for a while, are all too aware of the likely outcome. They need support in much the same way as would a patient with cancer, but they are unlikely to get it. Not only are the medical and nursing staff whom they meet determined to cure them, but any suggestion that this may not be possible is seen as defeatism.

The conflict is most clearly seen in relation to the decision to resuscitate, which does, at least, provide us with an opportunity to consider whether or not we are doing the patient a favour. Wherever it is reasonable to do so, we should discuss with our patients whether or not it is their wish that they be subjected to this painful procedure, preferably before the need arises. Very elderly patients or those whose illness is justifiably regarded as 'terminal' will often opt for a peaceful exit. But it is not sufficient for us to write 'Not for Resuscitation' on the notes and pass on. Once patients have been identified as unrecoverable we should treat them in much the same way as we would those in the late stages cancer, giving to them and their families the emotional support which will enable them to make something good of the time that remains to them.

Old age is not, of course, a terminal illness, but geriatricians make a valid distinction between 'young old age' and 'old old age'. The 'young old' still have a life to look forward to, whereas it is unrealistic for the 'old old' to make plans. The latter are more likely to spend their time looking back than forwards and will often find it hard to keep a grip on the things that are going on outside their immediate world. This disengagement, which in younger people would be a sign of depression, is a way of coping with a world that is getting too complex and which holds little promise for the future. Caregivers are sometimes tempted to cajole old people out of their withdrawal but this is not the kindest thing to do if they are in fact approaching the end of their lives.

HIV infection

Although the pattern of HIV/AIDS is changing, it is still true to say that many of those who contract it are psychologically vulnerable people, and were so even before the illness arose. Some have suffered the long-standing stigma attached to homosexuality, some are users of hard drugs, some are prostitutes; others will have lived in countries in which there is a high mortality from the disease, or will be people who have suffered for years from chronic blood diseases and been treated with contaminated blood products. Many will have partners, relatives or friends who have infected them or whom they have infected. This complicates their relationship with the people to whom most of us turn when we are in trouble.

The disease itself often remains dormant for many years before it becomes active. It then takes a very unpredictable course, so that it is hard for patients to know what plans it is reasonable for them to make. For many years they have to live with uncertainty, with the knowledge that they are a sexual hazard to others and with the stigma that they will face if it becomes known that they are HIV positive. Some choose to conceal the fact of their illness, but this too creates problems.

While modern methods of treatment for HIV infection have extended the life of many sufferers, it has also meant that those who survive long enough often become demented in the final phase of the illness. Patients know this and are understandably frightened at the prospect. Other symptoms which may occur in the later stages and which are difficult to treat are chronic, painful diarrhoea, painful ulcers in the mouth (thrush) and unsightly skin lesions. Small wonder that patients view the progress of the disease with considerable dread.

As in the case of cancer, the relationship between the patient and caregivers is all important. Patients need to know that we shall be available to help when needed, that we can be trusted to use every means to alleviate their symptoms and that our support will not flag. People with AIDS are very sensitive to rejection and it is no surprise to find that the person to whom many HIV-positive people turn for help is someone whom they see as like themselves. Buddy systems have been set up by a number of organizations supporting people with AIDS. Some of these use only gay men to support gay men. Other buddy systems, such as the OXAIDS buddies, include people from all walks of life, many of whom are neither gay nor men. Although this help is often very effective, many of those who offer their help in this way, particularly if they are members of a high-risk group, become multiply bereaved and overloaded. Some of them 'burn out', become depressed and withdraw. As in all counselling services, it is important to monitor the stress on the buddies as well as the clients and to make sure that nobody takes on more than they should.

Summary

❏   Many people with cancer move, in time, from a state of relative unawareness of their situation to a greater degree of 'acceptance'.

❏   Denial, anger, bargaining, depression and acceptance often occur but not necessarily consistently or in sequence.

❏   Styles of coping influence the way people respond to terminal illness. 'Thinkers' value independence and self-control; they often see emotional expression as a weakness and have difficulty in accepting help from others. 'Feelers' value cooperation, humility and respect for others; they sometimes depend too much on others and lack confidence in themselves.

❏   'Confrontation' and 'avoidance' of painful realities are normal reactions to trauma and usually alternate. Either may predominate as a coping style. Avoidance can become problematic if it leads to postponement of necessary planning, massive repression of emotion or if the effort required to maintain avoidance interferes with other psychological functioning. Confrontation can become problematic if it leads to obsessive preoccupation with loss or its consequences and withdrawal from other important activities.

❏   Breaking bad news requires time, planning, sensitivity and a proper place. We should to attempt to provide a secure base and a level of trust which will enable clients to explore the thoughts that make them feel insecure.

❏   We should respect people's coping strategies as long as they are effective and should not attempt to force people to cope in a particular way because we favour that strategy.

❏   To many patients, cancer means death in agony and it may come as a great surprise and relief to them to learn that this is not to be the case.

❏   Fear causes its own symptoms, which can be misinterpreted as signs of cancer. All pain is aggravated by fear and it is important for the physician to treat the fear as well as the pain.

❏   People who are coming to the end of their lives often experience grief; this may be expressed as anger, self-reproach, with guilt and loss of self-esteem, pining, and depression.

❏   Patients who become too depressed to grieve may need antidepressant medication. It is wise to choose the less toxic forms.

❏   Although suicide is rare among cancer patients it does sometimes occur and caregivers should assess the risk of suicide whenever they meet a patient who is unusually depressed or agitated.

❏   Staff should do all in their power to minimize the chances that patients will die alone.

❏   Children with cancer regularly know more about their illness than their parents imagine.

❏   People with AIDS are very sensitive to rejection and the person to whom many turn for help is someone whom they see as like themselves.

5

Counselling the Patient's Family Before Bereavement

In this chapter we start by considering how our traditional roles colour our attitude to the patient's family and by suggesting how we can counter some of the problems that arise from this. It is important for family members to be prepared for the losses that are to come and we discuss the care that is needed by most adults and children as the patient comes closer to death. We then go on to consider how to assess and manage particular needs. The genogram is a useful tool which helps us to assess the needs of the family and makes us aware of any special risks that exist. These risks may result from the circumstances of the illness and death or from the relationship with the person who is dying. Each is considered in turn along with its implications for counselling the family.

Our Attitude to the Family

Before we can become effective counsellors to the family, we may need to take stock of our own attitude and habits of thought about them. Most members of the caregiving professions have come to view their clients in particular ways which may not always be helpful. The very fact of identifying certain people as 'patients' places them at a distance from ourselves. This may be helpful if it enables us to be objective but it easily becomes a problem if it creates a barrier to communication or prevents us from seeing their point of view. It may also encourage us to be possessive, treating the patient as an object of care rather than a fellow human being who is in trouble.

Our perception of the family is different. We may speak of a patient as 'my patient' but we do not think of the family as 'my family'. The fact that we feel possessive towards 'our' patients may put us in conflict with the family, who also tend to think of the patient as 'theirs'. We are also possessive of 'our ward' and 'our treatments' and may resent the way in which family members intrude and compete with us. To keep the family at a safe distance we may introduce rules to limit their encroachment: restrictions on length and times of visits, obstacles in the way of doctors and unwritten but nonetheless powerful expectations that they will behave in a suitably submissive and respectful way. Even in those units where family members are not seen as intruders, they must talk softly, be polite and not get in the way of the doctors and nurses. These expectations, while not unreasonable, make it unlikely that the family will feel 'at home' in the hospital or see themselves as having a significant continuing role to play in the care of the patient.

These types of problem are less likely to arise while the patient is at home. Here we are the guests and the family 'own' the patient and the territory. But even in this setting it is only too easy for professionals to adopt possessive or authoritarian attitudes. If we feel no respect for the family, we are likely to treat them as incompetent and to make them feel incompetent. By subtly undermining their confidence, we may deskill them at a time when they need all the skills they possess in order to cope with the demands of caring for someone who is dying.

It follows that one of the most important things we have to offer the family is our respect for them. We are there to supplement the help which they are giving rather than to supplant them. We do this by listening, accepting and encouraging, as described in Chapter 3. We exist to support them and should take over from them only when it is clear that they need a break or that we have special skills which they need us to use on their behalf.

Having said this, there are also times when we may need to adopt overtly 'paternal' or 'maternal' roles, providing the family with advice as well as the support and reassurance that will make them feel secure enough to continue to cope with the enormous difficulties and dangers that they face. This is no time for lofty detachment: we have to get our hands dirty, to get into the thick of things with the family and to give them all the verbal and non-verbal encouragement that will enable them to get through.

There is no one attitude that we should adopt; rather, we need to become empathically aware how our behaviour is affecting the family so that it is their ever-changing needs that we are meeting, rather than our own. Of course, in the long run, professional carers have to meet their own needs too, and we discussed ways of doing this in Chapter 2. However, our first consideration will always be our patients and their families, and we may well find that, if we are successful in mitigating their pain and maintaining their functioning, things will get easier for us too.

Emotional Inoculation

Given the fact that everyone has to die of something, one of the good things about those illnesses (such as cancer) that enable us to predict when a person will die is that they give the family of the dying person time to prepare themselves for that event. One of the bad things is that the family often fail to take this opportunity.

There is much evidence that people who have anticipated a loss and begun the process of 'emotional inoculation' (sometimes termed 'anticipatory grieving') cope better with bereavement than those who have undergone no such preparation (Parkes, 1996). They find the shock of bereavement much less traumatic and are less likely to be haunted by painful memories and feelings of self-reproach than those who have suffered unexpected losses. It follows that we should do all in our power to ensure that, whenever possible, people whose lives will be affected by a death are warned of the danger and given any emotional support that they need in order to come to terms with it.

Support given to the family is support given to the patient; both will benefit and each will then be better able to support the other. It is tragic how often family members think that the best way of helping each other is by concealing or minimizing the seriousness of the illness. This is done with the best of intentions. If my wife does not know that I have cancer, she will not get upset and we shall both be happier. This kind of avoidance may work in the earlier stages of the illness, when there is a reasonable chance of a cure, but it will become an increasingly dubious policy as time goes by, and there will eventually come a time when my wife is more worried by *not* knowing where she and I stand than by knowing the truth. At least it will then be clearer what needs to be done. This is not to say that the widow-to-be immediately starts withdrawing herself and planning for her life after her husband's death. Unlike the grieving that takes place after a death, the anticipation of the death of a loved person tends to draw the parties closer together rather than to undo their attachment to each other. There are many bereaved people who will look back on the last few weeks or months of their life with their partner and say, 'We were never closer'. Minor differences and rivalries seem insignificant, sins of omission or commission are forgiven and each tries to make the best of the time that remains to them. Those who are facing the death of a loved person know that they have not got long to get things right. They know that they must sacrifice their own needs to those of the patient so that later they will be able to look back and say, 'I did everything possible.' The dying person may be cantankerous, self-centred and, at times, intolerable; but the family cannot afford the luxury of a tantrum for they know that any such outburst will linger in their memory as a source of shame for the rest of their lives: 'I let him down when he needed me most.' They are on their best behaviour and commonly attempt to conceal from the nurse or doctor, as well as the patient, the terrible stress which they are under.

To help the family through this crucial time in their lives, we must understand and show them that we understand the cruel obligations that the situation places upon them. We must give them every opportunity to provide the care that is needed, but recognize the burden that this places on them and ensure that it remains within their capacity. They must not fail, and we need to know if they are coming close to the end of their tether. We need to know the precise moment when we must encourage them to relinquish care to us, for a while, and the moment when they are capable of renewing the burden of care. This is most obvious when we are deciding whether or not to offer respite care, but it applies equally to other circumstances of inpatient and home care when we need to do something that might otherwise be done by a family member. While we obviously cannot and should not see ourselves as a part of the family, we do need to provide something of the same kind of commitment and care that one can expect of a family but without losing our objectivity or burdening them with our needs for care.

The Approach of Death

It is important for staff to alert the family when the patient is deteriorating and may not live much longer. This gives them time to gather and support one another. Our role at this time is to recognize and respect the uniqueness of their situation, keep them informed, involve them in the care of the patient whenever possible and appropriate, and explain the purpose of medication and other interventions. It is important to remember that the family will be under great stress and may not be able to take in or understand what we say. For this reason it is important not to give more information at a time than they can take in and to check what has been understood. From the family's point of view our presence at their side is a great source of reassurance. They will probably be feeling scared, helpless and deeply concerned. They may never before have witnessed a death, let alone that of someone they love. They have no idea what they should do or say in the face of this momentous event. 'Will the dying person cry out in death agonies?', 'Will I faint or go mad?', 'Will I lose control and rush screaming from the ward?' . These types of fantasy are commonly on the mind of family members and friends at the bedside of a person who is dying. It helps if we anticipate some of these worries. We may, for example, ask questions which will help people voice some of their fears: 'Have you been close by when someone died? ... What was that like for you?' Our empathy shows that we understand.

The family and friends watch apprehensively for signs of distress. The accumulation of secretions in the respiratory tract of an unconscious patient often gives rise to bubbling sounds, the 'death rattle', which, although it cannot worry the patient, may cause anxiety in those at the bedside: 'What has gone wrong? We thought it would be peaceful!' Reassurance that the patient is not suffering and an injection of hyoscine to reduce the secretions will often mitigate these fears.

Children

Children need to be included in the family's preparation for the death of a parent when death can be anticipated. They will know that something serious is happening and it is right to warn them that the person they love is very ill and that everything possible is being done by the nurses and doctors to make that person feel better. Parents will usually want to do this themselves and it is their responsibility to do so, but they will often delay in the vain hope that the situation will improve. Most, however, are willing to take advice from us and there is no harm in asking them what the children have been told and, if necessary, gently reminding them that they may not have much longer to prepare them. When it is clear that death is approaching, it is better to tell the children that the treatment is not working. A warning like, 'You know, I don't think mummy is going to come home from hospital,' will often provoke the question, 'Do you mean mummy is not going to get better?' This allows the answer, 'No, I think that she is going to die.' It is important to reassure children that nothing which they did has caused the illness, since young children often assume that everything that happens to them is caused by them. The children, who are very realistic about such things, may then ask, 'Who is going to look after us?' Whether or not they ask this question, it is important to attempt to reassure them by, for example, inviting the well parent to join in the conversation and tell them what plans have been made.

Very small children lack the patience to wait at the bedside of a dying person and inhibit others from acting in a relaxed and spontaneous way; they may also be frightened by the strange events and the behaviour of distraught adults. For these reasons it is not usually a good idea to encourage their presence at the moment of death. Older children, on the other hand, will often cope well and prefer to be allowed to remain at the bedside.

The Genogram

The first step in helping a family is to get to know them and this is facilitated by drawing a genogram. A genogram is a diagram of a family, a family tree, a form of shorthand by which a picture of a family can be written down and shared with others. It needs to be drawn at the time of first contact with the family and updated whenever new information comes to our notice. To the doctor, nurse, psychologist or social worker who is caring for a family, the genogram is one of the most important tools at our disposal. It is worth taking the trouble to learn the simple rules that govern their use and to use them frequently.

The act of drawing a genogram does two things. It informs us of the nature of the family that we are hoping to help and it demonstrates to the informant our interest in the family. Patients may be surprised to be asked about their families – it is not the kind of thing in which doctors and nurses usually take an interest – but they are reassured by that interest. They know only too well what a strain their illness is placing on their family. They may feel too ill or anxious to give support themselves, but they are glad to know that we are willing to become involved. 'I'm so worried about my wife. She had this awful depression after she lost that second baby, even threatened to kill herself, and I'm afraid she'll go right to pieces when I die.' Or 'Chrissie is the baby of the family; I've always been very close to her. Her mother's a wee bit jealous. They don't get on too well.' Revelations of this kind clue us into situations that may have many consequences before and after the patient's death. If problems emerge it is tempting for us to think that they are not our business; however, assessing the family's needs is very important since we can help with some of them and, even if we are not in a position to meet all these needs ourselves, there may well be other caregivers who can.

Drawing a genogram may not put us in control of the situation and there may be nothing which we can do to change it, but at least it will help us understand the problems we meet. Ward and home care teams will find it useful to have a flip chart to hand during ward rounds with a genogram of each family who is to be discussed.

If you are familiar with genograms we suggest that you miss out the next section and continue on page 105. If not, take a few minutes to examine Fig. 5.1, noting the ways in which men and women are depicted and each generation is on a different line. Observe the different links between ordinary siblings and twins, and the links between married partners and those who are cohabiting. Note that patients are normally denoted by a diagonal cross over their symbol and those who have died are blacked out.

This is the basic genogram and a great deal of extra information can be added to it as it becomes known. Cats and dogs are

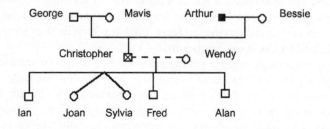

Figure 5.1 An example of a genogram.

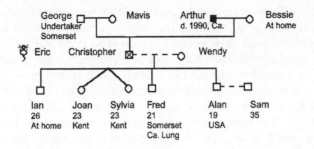

Figure 5.2   An elaborated genogram.

important members of some families and you can easily invent your
own symbols for them. Years of birth, death and marriage are
usually added. If you write in a current age remember that it will
have to be changed if the record is kept for over a year! Causes of
death, occupation and where each person lives are all useful data
which can be added. Some people draw in zig-zag lines to indicate
conflicts or double lines for very intense or dependent relationships, but these easily confuse the picture and are best added in a
different colour. Your finished genogram will probably end up
looking something like Fig. 5.2.

As an exercise we suggest that you break off at this point to draw
a genogram of your own family. Other examples of genograms will
be given elsewhere in this book.

The Assessment of Risk

The genogram helps us to begin the process of assessing the
vulnerability of all relevant family members. This is an important
task that needs to be taken seriously. It may require us to ask
personal questions and must be carried out with sensitivity and
tact. If people resent our questions or find them intrusive, we
should break off at once, but most people welcome our interest
and tell us a great deal more than we had thought to ask.

Some teams use formal questionnaires or scoring sheets in order
to assess risk. These were first introduced in St Christopher's
Hospice, Sydenham, in 1969, where they were originally used to
record information about the principal family member (or 'key
person'). Subsequently they were expanded to cover all family

members likely to be at risk and to include some general questions about the family as a whole. They are now used routinely in many hospices. Because their prime function is to assist staff in deciding which families will need help after bereavement, some hospices fill them in only after the patient's death. This, however, is illogical, since the assessment of risk begins as soon as we meet the family, and the sooner we become aware of any problems that exist, the better. For this reason risk assessment should be part of the case record, which is initiated at the point of contact with the service. This is then checked and completed at the time of the patient's death. Formal methods of assessment have the advantages of ensuring that a proper assessment of family need is being made and of reminding us of the issues that are likely to be important, and they are useful research tools.

The disadvantage of scoring sheets is that they interfere with spontaneous expression and cannot possibly cover the enormous range of possible risk factors. If they are to be used, it is important to make them an inconspicuous aid to questioning, rather than to engage in a formal ritual of reading the questions and scoring the answers. People should be encouraged to talk around the issues raised by the questions and their replies recorded or summarized in the notes. A telling comment, recorded word for word, can often

Table 5.1. *Factors influencing the response to death and bereavement*

Traumatic circumstances	Problematic relationships	Vulnerable people
Unexpected death	Unusually close, dependent or interdependent	Over-anxious people
Untimely death	Unusually conflicted	Depressive people
Painful or horrific death	Childless couples	Drug or alcohol abusers
Multiple losses	Insecure attachments	Insecure people
Stigma (e.g. with AIDS)	Young children	Aggressive people
	Adolescents	People with other personality or psychiatric problems
	Parents losing a child	
	Dysfunctional or unsupportive families	
	Secrets impairing communication	

'bring alive' the nub of a problem better than our own inter-
pretation of what the person is saying.

Whether or not we use a formal method of assessment we must
be aware of the factors that tend to make people vulnerable to
psychological problems after bereavement. These have emerged
from research, and the reader who wants to learn more about the
grounds for including them here may wish to read Parkes (1996).

As indicated in Table 5.1, vulnerability is influenced by: the
circumstances in which the patient is dying (some deaths are more
traumatic than others); the type of relationship between the patient
and the family member being assessed; and their personal characteristics. In addition, vulnerability is influenced by the type of
support which the family members receive, or fail to receive, from
those around them. Each of these carries its own implications for
counselling, so that routine assessment of risk also suggests the
type of support that may be needed before and after bereavement.

Traumatic circumstances

Untimely deaths for which we are unprepared, and multiple deaths
in a short space of time, easily tax the strength and resilience of the
strongest person. Even when a death has been anticipated, the
course of the final illness is all important. Memories of great
suffering or unrelieved pain will stick in our minds and embitter
us. Conversely a peaceful death is much easier to accept than a
distressed one.

Losses for which people are unprepared commonly cause them
to feel overwhelmed and out of control. Information or reminders
of the situation aggravate this feeling and may be so painful that
people try to avoid them, shutting themselves away or keeping so
busy that they cannot think. They may find it difficult to relax for
fear of the thoughts that will well up if they do. The more they try
to avoid painful thoughts the more these tend to sneak up on them.
This adds to the feeling of helplessness and loss of control.

It is important for helpers to realize that there is seldom any
point in trying to force people to confront painful facts. Attempts to
do so will only make them more anxious. They may then run away
by avoiding us or find some other way of shutting out the problem.
Rather, we should set out to reassure them of their own strength
and make them feel secure enough to begin to tackle the problems
they have been avoiding. On the other hand if, for instance, time is
very short, it may be necessary to be more active in warning people

that they do not have much time left to say 'goodbye'. This kind of message needs to be accompanied with extra support, as it is very likely to lead to severe distress. Other members of the family may need to be included.

Multiple bereavements or other traumatic life events all occurring close to each other can also overwhelm people's ability to cope. No sooner have they begun to come to terms with one loss when another comes about. It is easy to understand why people who suffer an overload of losses easily give up and become depressed and withdrawn. If we suspect that a family are on the point of 'burning out', admitting the patient to a hospital or hospice for respite care will often give them the break they need in order to regain control.

John was dying and Grace felt that her world was coming to an end. A year ago she had a family. Now both her children had finished their schooling and had left home, one to study and one to travel. She and John had planned for his retirement and looked forward to having more time together. Now all their plans were obsolete and the future appeared bleak and empty. Grace felt that as long as John lived she would have a purpose in her life. She urged him to eat when he no longer felt able to, begged the doctors not to give him medication that would make him drowsy and expressed extreme anxiety about any change in his condition. The social worker noticed Grace's anxiety and asked her what support she was getting from her family and friends. Grace found herself pouring out her fears that her friends would not want her without John and that her children, who had their own lives to lead, would find her a nuisance. The social worker reflected this back to her, saying, 'You are losing the key pivots of your life all at the same time. John's illness is cheating you of all your plans and you feel as if the future has little to offer.' Grace agreed that this was the case and was glad to accept the offer of further counselling. This helped her to prepare herself for John's death and continued afterwards as she struggled to build a new identity.

In such cases it is important to recognize that what the family member needs most is time: time to take in, little by little, the reality of what is happening, and time to work through the process of grieving. If we set up regular counselling meetings at which they can express their feelings to an uncritical listener and digest the information they need in 'bite-sized chunks', they will usually begin to prepare themselves for what is to come.

Problems arise if the patient's illness is progressing too fast for us to give people the time they need. In this case there may be little we can do to prevent the trauma except to remind them that nobody can take in or deal with more than one thing at a time, and to help them to decide what are the vital things that must be faced now and what can be set aside until there is more time. In such circumstances denial and avoidance are not problems to be tackled but ways of coping with an otherwise impossible situation.

Barbara felt abandoned when her husband was discharged home to die. He left the hospital on Friday night with the promise that home care would be arranged but was in such severe pain over the weekend that she called in the GP's deputizing service. The doctor was reluctant to change the medication and, although the hospice's home care nurse arrived on the Monday, it was too late to get the pain fully controlled before his death on the following day.

Barbara felt understandably bitter about the circumstances and it was most important to her that her complaints were taken seriously and a proper inquiry held into the circumstances of her husband's death.

Because many traumatic bereavements are caused by sudden or unexpected deaths there may be little that can be done to mitigate them before the bereavement. We shall, therefore, delay further discussion of them to the next chapter, in which we shall consider the counselling that is needed after bereavement.

Physical mutilation, haemorrhages, foul smells and purulent discharges all add to the trauma of the death of a loved person and every effort should be made to minimize, control and, where necessary, conceal them. When they cannot be concealed the adoption of a matter-of-fact rather than an alarmist or over-concerned attitude on the part of the staff makes it easier for the family to do the same. Mutilation is often harder for the onlooker than the patient, but even the most extreme can become 'ordinary' if it is permitted to do so.

A child of five gazed apprehensively at the face of a patient in a hospice. 'Why haven't you got no nose mister?' he said. The patient, who was used to his appearance, laughed and said, 'A dicky bird pecked it off.' A few minutes later the child's mother walked into the ward to find her little boy sitting happily on the lap of the man with no nose. She did not need anyone to tell her that there was nothing wrong.

Relationships that cause problems

The commonest of these are unusually close or unusually conflicted relationships with the patient. *Unusually close relationships* are easy to recognize: insecure family members are inseparable from the dying person and intolerant of separation. They anxiously seek reassurance from doctors and nurses, telephone at all hours of the day and night, and communicate their fears to everyone, including the patient. Their own wish for support may blind them to the similar needs of the patient, who may be unable to cope with their clinging. It is clear that these people are emotionally dependent individuals who have little confidence in themselves. When things went wrong in the past they have turned to the patient for support, and the thought that he or she may not remain available to them provokes an intense and panicky desire to cling all the tighter. Another cause of unusual closeness may be childlessness. When a couple have no children they may focus all their affection on each other. If they lack a supportive network, one may nurse the other devotedly at times of sickness, but when serious illness arises may become extremely anxious and despairing.

To staff, this tendency to anxiety and clinging is seen as a threat to our attempts to reassure 'our' patients and create an atmosphere in which they can die a peaceful death. It is tempting to take over the entire care of the patient, blame the family members for their 'weakness' and to adopt a 'pull yourself together' attitude towards them. Such a reaction will only make them feel all the more anxious and insecure and may even aggravate their tendency to cling.

If, on the other hand, we recognize their behaviour for what it is – a sign of their own concern and fear – and if we treat them with respect and courtesy, we may find them very responsive. We cannot give them what they most want – reassurance that the patient will get better – but we can give them reassurance of their own strength. We do this by asking for their opinions and their help whenever this is reasonable, by rewarding with a smile or a hug any positive contribution which they make to the care of the patient, and by taking over only those aspects of care which are clearly too much for them. In this way a fruitful collaborative relationship with the family can be developed which will stand them in good stead later, when they need to be able to say, 'I did everything possible'.

Unusually conflicted relationships may not be so easy to identify. Family members often put on a show for the doctors and nurses whom they meet and will do their best to conceal any tensions between them. Only when they begin to trust us will they admit the true situation. When one or other loses their temper we may be surprised at the intensity of the rage and resentment that boils up.

It is important to recognize that few relationships are totally hostile; ambivalence, a mixture of love and hate, is much more common. This explains the fact that a couple who appear to hate each other stay together or soon return after any period of separation. Often one or other partner has learned early in life that closeness is dangerous. Things begin to go wrong when some unusual stress causes one or other partner to lean on the other, only to find that the other feels too insecure to reciprocate.

It is, of course, much easier to hurt people you love than people you hate. The very closeness that was so rewarding in the early days of the relationship may become a threat when it is used to get behind your defences. 'She is so intrusive – never lets me have a thought of my own,' or, 'He brings up all the confidences that we have shared and quotes them against me.'

When an intimate relationship goes wrong, couples often feel the need to turn for support to someone outside the relationship. This may cause further trouble, particularly if that relationship becomes sexual. 'I knew it was a stupid thing to do, but I felt so angry with her that I didn't care.' When the partner becomes aware of the 'betrayal', this confirms worst fears about the relationship and aggravates the distrust. Despite this the couple often remain attached, vainly seeking for proof of love, yet unwilling to accept any reassurance that the other person attempts to give.

Conflicted relationships often result from and aggravate pre-existing feelings of insecurity. Two insecure, ambivalent people, who may have grown up with little trust in others, are often attracted because they understand each other. For a while they may tolerate their partner's distrust because they understand it. But such relationships are often punctuated by episodes of mutual hostility, when one or other partner gets to the end of their tether.

Terminal illness introduces another powerful element into ambivalent relationships. It may further undermine security and unbalance a precarious adjustment; 'Just when I needed him most he backed away. I felt very let down.' On the other hand, cancer may also change the situation in positive ways. Sickness may provide the very opportunity that partners need to show that they care. Given a little encouragement, devoted care may be given and old antagonisms and betrayals be set aside. Each partner has something important to offer to the other and it is up to us to make it as easy as possible for them to give it. We should not deprive them of the opportunity to care, even if we think we can care better.

In all our dealings with families it is important for us to remain strictly impartial. Our natural inclination may be to side with one or other partner. As caregivers we can easily identify with other caregivers and may find ourselves taking sides with a wife who is looking after a difficult husband or a mother whose child is being unreasonable. If we do that we will often be surprised how easy it is to find ourselves drawn into family quarrels that have been going on for years and, having taken one side, we are very likely to be rejected by the other ('I might have guessed: you women always stick together'). Support comes from understanding rather than agreeing.

Overcoming Reluctance to be at the Bedside

Genograms tell us about the *people who do not visit* as well as the ones who do. Sometimes this may reflect hostility, but it is more likely to reflect fear. The fear may reside in patients who are afraid that family members will be disgusted or upset by seeing them, or it may reside in the family members who see hospitals as terrifying places.

George telephoned a social worker in great distress to explain that he could not find the courage to visit his wife, who was very ill with cancer in a nearby hospital. He had a phobia of hospitals. 'I don't know what to do,' he said. 'She doesn't understand that the very thought of sitting at her bedside brings me out in a sweat of fear. She thinks it means that I don't love her.' The social worker discussed the situation with him and reassured his wife that he did care and that his phobia of hospitals was the reason he could not visit. He also questioned George carefully about exactly what he felt and what he could, and could not, manage when visiting someone in hospital.

To clarify the situation, and enable improvement to be monitored, the social worker asked George to help him to measure his fear using a 10-point scale, with 10 representing the worst fear that George could imagine. The thought that if he visited his wife he would have to wait until the end of a visiting hour before he could escape was scored 9. The thought of entering the hospital and waving to his wife from the door of the ward before leaving straight away rated a score of 6, but this was reduced to 4 if he could be accompanied by his brother.

The social worker explained to George that the phobia was certainly not his fault and gave some suggestions about the ways in which he could try to control his anxiety and fear, as described on page 173. He suggested that George visit the ward with his brother and told him that on no account was he to go beyond the door of the ward or to stay for longer than it took to wave to his wife. The social worker then explained the plan to his wife, who was warned not to expect him to remain for more than a moment at the door of the ward.

In the event the plan worked very well. When George got to the door of the ward he discovered that he was not nearly as frightened as he had expected. Against the social worker's advice he sat by his wife's bed for ten minutes and went home feeling like a hero. His wife, his brother and the social worker had been very appreciative of his effort and, although he was still apprehensive, he could not wait to go back on the next day. His remaining fears soon evaporated and he was soon spending many hours each day at his wife's bedside.

Psychologists will recognize in this account the classic way of treating phobias by 'progressive desensitization'. But one does not have to be a psychologist to realize that fears can often be overcome by taking a 'little by little' approach. By reassuring George that he would not be trapped in the hospital and by respecting the intensity of his fear, the social worker was able to help him to work out a plan which enabled him to turn failure into success.

Children and people with learning difficulties are often excluded from the bedside in the mistaken belief that visiting someone in hospital will only upset them and it is kinder for them to be left at home. 'I wouldn't want them to see me like this' is a common remark which reflects the patient's feeling that he or she is no longer of any use to the children and might even harm them by causing them distress. The truth is that the children are far more likely to feel lasting distress and rejection by being excluded than they are to be upset by visiting. Their parent or other relative will soon be dead and this may be their last chance to express and receive love. Even if parents have succeeded in concealing the seriousness of the illness from the children, they cannot do this for ever. Sooner or later the children are bound to find out and it is better for them to be put in the picture while both parents are still available to help them through than it is to leave them in ignorance until one of them is dead.

Some dying parents have taken great pleasure in helping their child to put together a collection of valued objects, favourite books, photographs, jewellery and so on.

One eight-year-old boy kept what he called 'Mum's Box' by the side of the bed. His mother had helped him to decide what to put into it. When, after her death, he felt unwell, he would open it and show its contents to his grandmother so that, together, they could acknowledge how much they missed his mother. He always took the box with him when he went on holiday.

Children need to feel welcome on a ward. A play area is a valuable resource which provides them with a place to go when they get bored at the bedside. If this is not available, drawing materials and toys should be provided. If carefully chosen, these can help children to express some of their concerns through play. For example, 'doctors and nurses' sets, toy ambulances and hospital beds encourage children to communicate with us and provide staff with insight into their view of the situation.

Caring staff are in a position to support and advise patients regarding communication with their families and we can often help them to feel secure enough to risk upsetting people because they know that we are at hand to support them.

Family Homeostasis and Dysfunction

Much has been written about the family as a homeostatic unit. By this we mean that families develop a repertoire of ways of coping which tend to restore equanimity whenever upsets occur. Often leadership is focused on one person, who is expected to keep things in balance. If dangers arise, dad (or mum) will solve the problem and make things right again. In return the family are expected to cooperate with the leader and to follow his or her advice. Such families are particularly vulnerable if the leader becomes ill. In others, leadership is divided, with different family members performing different functions. Thus mother may be the one who is turned to at times of emotional conflict because she is warm and a good listener, while father may be better at 'getting things done'. Family therapists talk about 'family myths', the beliefs which govern the behaviour of the family and provide security. However, these work only so long as everyone believes them: they may cause big problems if faith in the system is lost. Illnesses often change the balance of power within a family, making it more difficult for leadership and other long-standing roles and assumptions to be maintained. When this happens the family may no longer be able to provide its members with the security they need. Some members, in trying to cling to roles that are no longer valid, may even aggravate the problem. At such times we speak of the family system as 'dysfunctional'.

Dick and Jane were like the police officers who share the interviewing of suspects by adopting extreme attitudes, one being aggressive and the other the 'nice guy'. In this case Dick was the tough guy, strong, dominant and effective; he made all the important decisions in the family and nobody dared to argue with him. Jane was loved by everybody; she was gentle, kind, affectionate and tolerant. She deferred to her husband in all things and saw him as the strong partner. In fact it was generally assumed that mother was 'nice but weak' while father was 'cold but strong'. Their three children, growing up in this family (Fig. 5.3), naturally assumed that what was normal for their family was normal for the world. Billy, the eldest, tried hard to live up to his father but knew that he could never quite succeed: by comparison with his dad he was a 'wimp'. The girls were both

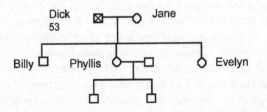

Figure 5.3   Genogram of Dick's dysfunctional family.

clever but did not make much use of their brains because they 'knew' that girls do not amount to much. Dick seemed to like being top dog and would become very angry and punitive if any of the family members disagreed with him or challenged his authority. His wife said, ruefully, 'He likes to be right and, quite frankly, he usually is.'

When Dick, at the age of 53, was found to have a carcinoma of the lung (he had seldom been seen without a cigarette in his mouth), the family was devastated. Dick struggled to maintain his position by denying that there was anything seriously wrong and insisting that he would soon be cured and back at work. The family colluded with him, but it was becoming increasingly obvious that he was no longer the man he had been. When he was admitted to the local hospice for pain control he had lost a great deal of weight and was very weak. He plummeted into depression and the family followed suit. His wife told the doctors that 'the heart has gone out of my family' and that she could see no way in which they could now survive. It seemed that the entire family was sick. Billy found himself unable to concentrate on his work and developed abdominal pains surprisingly similar to those from which his father was suffering. Phyllis, the second and the only married child, neglected her family in order to stay close to her parents. Her husband, who had always thought that she loved her father more than she loved him, threatened to leave and a major quarrel ensued which nearly destroyed their relationship and confirmed their view that this family was 'going to pieces'. Only Evelyn, the youngest, seemed relatively unscathed. She was in her last year at university and she buried herself in her work. She was criticized by her sister because she seldom visited her father, but her mother explained that this was all to the good because, as the baby of the family, she would never be able to cope if she did visit. Since they had never expected anything better of her she was permitted to withdraw.

The home care nurses had been aware of the problems in this family even before Dick was admitted to the hospice, but it was the nurses on the ward and the ward doctor and social worker who became most closely involved when morale in the family deteriorated after his admission. All of them happened to be women and Dick needed to learn that he could trust them to look after him and to support his family. The combination of an antidepressant and morphine with this psychosocial support soon brought his pain under control and, although he was never able to resume the dominant role which he had assumed in the past, Dick gradually became less depressed and was able to let go of the reins. Jane and Phyllis both needed to be given permission to take control of their own lives and indeed Jane surprised everyone by coping very well once she realized that her husband was very grateful for her presence at the bedside and that little more would be expected of her. Phyllis too, when she realized that there was nothing more that she could or should do to change her father's situation, worked out with her husband a compromise plan that enabled her to divide her attention between her parents, her husband and her own children without detriment to any of them. The social worker, with whom she developed a good relationship, helped her to realize that she was coping remarkably well, given the difficulties of the situation.

Evelyn, once she had completed her examinations and done rather well, began visiting the ward more frequently and was relieved to find that the atmosphere had changed and that she was not immediately sucked into the vortex of despair from which she had run away.

The most difficult person to help was undoubtedly Billy, who, according to the prevailing family myth, was now expected to take over the leadership role from his fast-dwindling father. Lacking the confidence to do this but determined to try to meet the expectations of the women in the family, he blustered and vacillated, making decisions which he would countermand the next day and oscillating between attempts at assertion and episodes in which he seemed more like a helpless child than 'the man of the family'. He found it difficult to ask for help but responded well when the chaplain (a man) gave him the opportunity to talk 'man to man' about his feelings of helplessness in the face of a trap from which he could see no escape. It was the chaplain who suggested that in fact the women of the family were coping perfectly well and that it might not be wise or necessary for him to encourage everybody to rely on him in the way that they had relied on his father.

In reaching out to dysfunctional families there is a limit to what we should expect to achieve. The problems may stem from habits that are far too deep-seated for us to alter. On the other hand, we should not assume that we have nothing to offer, but should take advantage of the fact that illness may create the very situation in which something *has* to change. Trusted people from outside the family may help the family to recognize that fact and provide them with the support they need to re-examine the family myths and to reach a new kind of adjustment.

Secrets in the Family

The process of dying and bereavement may be further complicated by secrets in the family. The family history will influence reactions to the current events and the readiness to trust professional or volunteer carers. If, for example, the dying or the bereaved person is involved in an extramarital affair, is a gay man or lesbian woman, has been the victim of incest or involved in other taboo sexual practices (such as sadomasochistic behaviour or cross-dressing) he or she may find it difficult to be open and at the same time may have issues that he or she very much wants to address.

Sally had been married to Bill, her second husband, for 15 years. Their marriage had been a source of great happiness to her, in contrast to her first marriage, which had ended in divorce. Sally and Bill had made his house their home. While Bill was in hospital Sally experienced bursts of restless energy and decided to sort through some old boxes in the attic. Among them she found old photographs of Bill in submissive poses with different women, together with leather clothes and whips. Sally felt as if the bottom had fallen out of her world. She went over and over in her mind her knowledge of Bill, trying to match the man she knew with the man in the photographs. She felt unable to talk to anyone and the thought of going to the hospital and seeing Bill very difficult. Nevertheless, she knew she must visit and decided to try to ignore the photographs, so that she could carry on supporting Bill in his illness, since the pictures all predated her relationship with him.

On her way into the ward, the charge nurse stopped her to tell her that Bill was less well. He noticed that Sally seemed pre-occupied and was not really listening to what he was saying. He asked, 'Has something happened today? You seem disturbed. Are you worried about Bill?' Sally looked at him and burst into tears. She said she could not talk about what was bothering her, but agreed to see the nurse again the following day during a quiet time on the ward. On this visit the nurse took her to a private room and explained that he had time and would not be called away. Sally plucked up the courage to talk about what had happened and how angry she was with Bill. The nurse listened and empathized with her feelings of bewilderment and how difficult it was for her. He helped her to think through whether to confront Bill or not. As he was so much more ill, she was adamant that he should not know she had found the photographs. The nurse thought about suggesting she see a social worker to carry on talking, but decided that it would be better for him to give support as he already had established a trusting relationship.

He saw her again a few days later and this time Sally asked the questions that were bothering her. Why had she not experienced this side of Bill? Might he have continued his masochistic practices in secret? Why had he kept the photographs? Did other men do such things? She found the nurse's comments on male sexuality reassuring. Bill was probably not as extreme in his behaviour as she had thought. Sally found that talking it over helped her to deal with her anger and carry on supporting Bill. He died two weeks later and Sally felt pleased that she had been able to honour her relationship with him.

Lesbians and gay men face the stigma attached to same-sex partnerships and are surrounded by misunderstanding. Their relationships may be secret to all but a few and they frequently mourn alone, the impact of their loss largely unrecognized. The advent of AIDS has heightened awareness of the needs of same-sex partners. Professionals working in hospices and hospital wards where there are many people who are HIV positive are likely to respond with greater empathy to the needs of the gay partner and the patient's family. However, lesbians and gay men facing bereavement from other causes are much less likely to meet such understanding.

It is important that health care professionals create an atmosphere in which people can be open about their relationships. Sometimes the doctors and nurses must take the initiative to make the partner feel accepted. It is very difficult to 'come out' at such a stressful time. Local lesbian and gay organizations are often willing to be involved in awareness training and to advise how institutions can make it easier for people to feel more able to be open.

Lesbians and gay men may have to cope with concurrent stresses. The patient may have kept his or her sexual preference secret, or the family may have been unable to accept the situation. The family of origin may try to exclude the partner; even if the partner is named as the next of kin, in some countries blood relatives may legally override this. If this happens the nurse involved is in the best position to negotiate between the partner and the family, recognizing the needs of all.

After the patient's death the partner may face acrimony over what happens to possessions and may lose his or her home. If the patient is a parent, there may be a struggle with the family or social services about whether or not the child should continue to live with the partner. These concurrent crises may cause the partner to feel overwhelmed, misunderstood and isolated. People who suffer rejection and alienation may come to believe that they are worthless. It is important that we try to redress the balance by treating them with the affection and respect that are the right of every human being.

Deaths from AIDS

If patients are dying from AIDS, they may conceal their diagnosis from their parents or other members of the family, and staff members have to be very careful not to break confidence. In such cases it is important to agree with the patient how we should respond to questions and to arrange for all questions to be dealt with by the same staff member. It is usually possible to give an explanation of the illness in such cases that is true without being the whole truth.

In most cases of AIDS, the diagnosis is obvious to everyone and there is little point in attempting to hide it. A young homosexual man who becomes seriously ill will always arouse suspicion of AIDS, as will a known abuser of injectable drugs. Friends and relatives may collude with the patient to pretend that they do not know the diagnosis. This may reduce embarrassment but it also inhibits spontaneous communication and impairs the ability of family and friends to give the support that is needed. On the other hand, the person with AIDS who chooses to reveal the diagnosis will usually find family and friends supportive, but not always; the fear and stigma evoked by AIDS are such that major family quarrels may occur and some people find themselves ostracized.

Members of the caring professions can often help by educating family and friends about AIDS. They need to know that it cannot be communicated by touching or other non-sexual contact. Sexual partners need to be given the opportunity to take a blood test, for they are at risk. All are now expected to receive counselling from a trained person before taking the test and it is advisable for us to leave it to the specialist counsellor to help them to decide whether or not to go ahead with this.

Some people with AIDS may have family problems that precede the illness. Gay men may have been rejected by their parents, who see their sexuality as abhorrent or a reproach to them as parents. Gay partners are likely to be under severe stress. They themselves may be HIV positive and view with personal apprehension the deterioration of their lover. They may find it difficult to provide the necessary care because of their own fears, anger or guilt. People involved in the misuse of drugs may similarly have been rejected by, or have rejected, their family of origin. Haemophiliacs and hetero-sexuals may feel unable to share the diagnosis with their family because they fear that they will be rejected. The consequences of secrecy, rejection and fear of rejection, may be profound.

Michael lived in a city some 60 miles from his family of origin. He maintained loose contacts with them but shared little about his personal life or relationships. His parents described him as being 'a very quiet and private person' and, although wishing that they shared more, were reasonably happy that he had established a life of his own. When his father became terminally ill, Michael was supportive, visiting fairly often and telephoning regularly. His mother, Pamela, was horrified when one day he told her that he too had been diagnosed as having cancer. He said he did not want to talk about his illness and that she should not worry as he was quite well. He carried on as before over the next few months, avoiding any questions about his own health. However, after his father's death, Michael's visits and telephone calls began to tail off and two months later he wrote an angry letter to Pamela saying that he no longer wished to be in contact. She heard no more from him and he died eight weeks later without further contact. During this period Pamela began to suspect that he was suffering from AIDS and not cancer. Her other children refused to believe this was possible and she was able to explore her fears only with a counsellor. Michael died in his flat alone and his body was not found for several days. The post-mortem examination confirmed Pamela's suspicions. She was overwhelmed with sad-ness that her son felt that he must keep his disease a secret, and guilt that he should have such an undignified death. She had regrets that she knew so little about her son's life. She never knew whether he was heterosexual, gay or bisexual, although she suspected the last. However, certainly his relationships were secret from his family and his work colleagues. A year later she continued to work through her feelings and reactions with her counsellor.

It is surprising how much can be achieved if we are sufficiently open, flexible and caring enough to offer a secure base to help people explore their reactions. A counsellor who can be relied on to accept and treat a person with AIDS with respect and without judgement is of inestimable value.

Summary

☐ One of the most important things we have to offer the family is our respect for them. We exist to support them and should take over from them only when it is clear that they need a break or that we have special skills which they need us to use on their behalf.

☐ One of the good things about those illnesses (such as cancer) which enable us to predict when a person will die is that they give the family time to prepare themselves. One of the bad things is that the family often fail to take that opportunity.

☐ People who have anticipated a loss cope better with bereavement than those who have undergone no such preparation.

☐ Family members often think that the best way of helping each other is by concealing or minimizing the seriousness of the illness.

☐ Family members commonly attempt to conceal from the nurse or doctor, as well as the patient, the terrible stress which they are under.

☐ When the patient is approaching death our role is to keep the family informed, support them emotionally, involve them in the care of the patient whenever appropriate and explain the purpose of medication and other interventions.

☐ Children need to be included in the family's preparation for the death of a parent.

☐ A genogram should be drawn at the time of first contact with the family and updated whenever new information comes to our notice.

☐ The routine assessment of risk is useful as a means of determining who needs help and it suggests the type of support that may be needed before and after bereavement.

☐ Vulnerability is influenced by the circumstances in which the patient is dying, the type of relationship between the patient and the family members being assessed, their personal characteristics and the type of support which they receive, or fail to receive, from those around them.

☐ If the patient's illness is progressing too fast for us to give people the time they need, we should remind them that nobody can take in or deal with more than one thing at a time and to help them to decide what are the vital things that must be faced now and what can be set aside until there is more time.

☐ It is important that health care professionals create an atmosphere in which people can be open about their relationships.

☐ Members of the caring professions can often help by educating family and friends about AIDS.

☐ In cases of HIV infection the consequences of secrecy, rejection and fear of rejection may be profound. Much can be achieved if we are sufficiently open, flexible and caring to offer a secure base to help people explore their reactions.

6

Counselling the Family after Bereavement

In this chapter we turn to the support that is needed after bereavement. We describe the care required at the time of, and in the immediate aftermath of, the death and suggest that this should be provided by people already known to the bereaved person. We then outline the indications for bereavement counselling and describe a practical framework for helping bereaved people. Consideration of some of the special problems of bereaved people will be covered in the chapter that follows.

The support that bereaved people may need differs as time passes. Two phases will be considered:

(1) the initial, *impact*, phase, which lasts from the moment of death until the initial numbness is past, the funeral is over and the family (who will normally have rallied round) have dispersed – a period of about three weeks;

(2) the phase of *adjustment*, which continues throughout the first year and beyond, depending on the type of bereavement. It is during the adjustment phase that bereavement counselling is most often needed.

Phase I. Impact

During the impact phase, care most often needs to be given by the same people who have looked after the patient and family before the death: the extended family and friends backed by the familiar primary care team and, where possible, hospital or hospice staff. If, however, care is needed during the impact phase but is not available, perhaps because there are no friends or family, or the medical/nursing team do not consider it part of their role to support the bereaved, then it may be necessary to introduce a counsellor at this earlier stage.

When Hazel Danbury asked clients for their criticisms of the help they had received from local bereavement services, several complained that help had not been present when it was most needed, during the first few weeks after the bereavement (Danbury, 1996). It follows that bereavement counsellors should be flexible and should not hesitate to offer support if it is clear that this will not otherwise be given.

Only a minority of bereaved people will, however, need bereavement counselling and, as indicated in Chapter 5, the decision to offer counselling should be made only after a systematic assessment of need.

Supporting the family at the time of death

The events surrounding the death of the patient will remain etched in the memories of the survivors. This is a time of crisis for the family, no matter how well prepared they are or think they are, and it is important that we respect this and do all that we can to minimize further distress and to provide the security and re-assurance needed by the family as they confront their loss.

Health care professionals need to be willing to share their vigil as the end approaches and to know what to do when the last breath has been taken. This is the moment when some people panic or become very distressed. We must be there to hold them, physically and emotionally, and to stay with them until their distress begins to subside. After a few minutes of silence, for there is nothing that has to be done immediately, some nurses find it helps to ask, 'Would you like me to say a prayer?' Even those families who have no strong religious faith may feel that a short prayer is fitting at so solemn a moment. An example of such a prayer reads:

Into Your Hands, O Merciful Saviour, we commend your servant. Receive him/her into your arms of mercy, into the blessed rest of your everlasting peace, and into the glorious company of the saints in light. AMEN

Family and friends should be permitted to stay with the patient's body for as long as they reasonably wish, preferably before it is removed to the mortuary. During this time people begin to take in the full reality of the fact of death and they should not be made to feel that we are in a hurry or that they are a nuisance. We can show by our own behaviour that it is safe to touch the dead person and should not discourage them from kissing or cuddling the dead person if they wish to do so. On occasion it may be appropriate for a relative to help wash and lay out the body. Again, we should use our counselling skills to tune into the uniqueness of each situation and to ensure that we do not impose our ideas of what is right on the family.

Christine was a bright 12-year-old who told the home care nurse that she had always wanted to become a nurse, 'But I'm not sure I could cope with people dying and all that.' Her father was dying at home from a long-standing cancer of the prostate and Christine helped her mother to look after him.

His death, when it came, was very peaceful. Christine and the nurse were present at the bedside and the nurse explained to her what had to be done and asked her if she would like to help.

When I (CMP) visited the home a few weeks later to check on the need for bereavement counselling Christine answered the door. She told me in detail about her father's death which, she said, had reassured her that she did not need to feel frightened about death. She was particularly proud of the fact that she had helped to lay him out and felt that this had been her last opportunity to care for her father. I had no doubt that the way in which she had been helped had enabled her to come to terms with her fears and to turn the death of her father into an opportunity for personal growth.

Not all young people would be capable of this level of achievement and it would, of course, be a mistake to press them to undertake tasks which they would view with horror. However, this case illustrates the extent to which a nurse's own attitude to her work can reassure others and help them to overcome their fears.

Given the awesomeness of the event it is not surprising that misunderstandings occur. Unless handled carefully these may have an adverse effect on the survivor's long-term wellbeing. One commonly held belief is that health care professionals, particularly those working in a hospice or hospital unit with a high death rate, will be able to predict the time of death with great accuracy. Unfortunately some patients die when exhausted relatives have left the bedside to have a few hours' rest or a meal. This may cause anger and guilt.

Mary was slowly dying. The nurses had informed her family and Joan, her daughter, was keeping vigil at her bedside. At midnight the night staff suggested that she take a break, reassuring her that they would call her if Mary's condition changed. Two hours later she became rapidly worse and she died while the nurse was fetching Joan from the relatives' overnight room. Joan was bitterly disappointed and very guilty at having let her mother down. She said: 'They know when people are dying. They stopped me from being with my mother and I will never forgive them, or myself for following their advice.'

Another common misunderstanding is that the staff have caused the patient's death by giving medication or other care.

Jim was dying. He was hot and sweaty and the nurses decided to give him a partial wash to make him more comfortable. The curtains were pulled round the bed and the nurses proceeded to wash him. At times he moaned and the family, hearing this, assumed he was very distressed. Jim died half an hour later. When she returned the next day his wife, Maria, questioned the nurses about the need to wash Jim. She was very upset and wanted to know whether it had caused him to die in pain. 'I heard him screaming in agony,' she said. 'You should have left him alone.' The nurse acknowledged Maria's anger and distress and explained that Jim died much faster than expected. Maria then went on to talk about her anxiety about Jim's death and his rapid deterioration: 'I just didn't have time to take in what was happening.' As she talked she began to think that perhaps his death was more peaceful than she remembered. The nurse regretted that she had not included Maria in the decision to wash Jim or given her the opportunity to participate.

If we feel that misunderstandings have been left unresolved, we should invite the family back to talk it through at a time that will suit them. It is important that this initiative comes from the staff involved; unless people are very angry they are unlikely to feel free to request a meeting.

Cultural diversity

We live in a multi-ethnic society and need to have a thorough understanding of the beliefs and rituals that accompany death in people whose backgrounds may differ from our own. In many faiths, such as orthodox Judaism and Buddhism, the presence of a religious leader at the bedside at the moment of death is all important and we should do our best to make this possible. They will tell us what more is needed. When no religious leader is available we should take our lead from the family. It is common practice in some cultures to wail loudly and, although this can be very disconcerting if it should happen on the wards of a hospital or hospice, it should be permitted. In such cases it is important to explain the situation to any other patients or families who may be distressed by the noise. They will be more tolerant if they understand that this is culturally normal behaviour.

Moslems may want to turn the face of the dying patient towards Mecca and to take responsibility for the body soon after death in order that the appropriate people can carry out the ritual washing. In this instance non-Moslem staff should avoid touching the body if at all possible and should not carry out the last offices unless the family have requested them to do so. For further details of the ways in which death and bereavement are handled in various cultures, see Parkes *et al.* (1996).

Viewing the body

Viewing the body is usually an experience that is beneficial rather than harmful. However, harm can occur and it is important for us to understand how this can happen so that we can minimize the risk. An opportunity to spend time with the dead person helps people to appreciate the fact that the person is really dead and, while this may be a painful realization, it reduces the chance that the bereaved will cling to an unrealistic hope that the person is not truly dead and is about to return.

People may be reluctant to view the body for a number of reasons. They may be frightened of being so close to death, they may imagine that the person will look ghastly, or they may have painful memories of a past death that had been mishandled or horrific. In such cases we should explore the reasons with them and help them to make an informed choice. Even if the family want to see the dead person it is important that we spend time preparing them.

It helps if we anticipate some of these worries. Above all we should give information to prepare people for what they will see. This is particularly important if the person was not present at the bedside at the time of death. The relaxation of the facial muscles which occurs after death usually produces an appearance of peace, which may contrast with any tension, fear or depression which preceded death. Consequently most people are reassured by what they see when they choose to view a dead person. The reality is much less horrific than the picture their imagination has projected.

The nurses called Noreen to say that her mother was dying, but she lived some distance away and by the time she arrived it was too late. Noreen immediately wanted to see her mother and was taken to the viewing room. The nurse noticed that she seemed very anxious and found her very distressed afterwards. However, she did not want to make it worse by asking questions. Some months later Noreen came to a fund-raising event. She arrived in tears saying, 'I don't know how I managed to come here again after how I was treated'. It transpired that she had felt badly let down. 'I had never seen a dead person before and I was so frightened. I had no idea how Mum would have been changed and the nurse just left me there. You should tell people what to expect and find out if they want someone with them. Death may be routine to you but it isn't to me.'

The main danger arises from the occasional persistence of horrific memories. This is most likely to occur if people are surprised by some unexpected mutilation or impression for which they were not prepared. An unpleasant smell, a bloody exudate or the visible or felt evidence of a post-mortem examination can cause a shock which will then remain imprinted on the mind. To prevent this it is important to prepare people. This is particularly important if relatives have had little or no opportunity to see the person before death and may not have been warned of the changes caused by the disease. In such cases it is wise to spend time explaining what they should expect. If the body has been badly disfigured it is advisable to cover up the most damaged parts and to warn people of the damage, but we should not prevent them from spending time with their dead relative.

Brian's wife died peacefully in the hospice. However, after her death her face seemed to change. Once the spark of life had departed the ravages of her months of illness could clearly be seen. Brian was disturbed by this and talked about the dramatic change with his sister. She informed him that this must mean that his wife's soul was being tormented in purgatory. Brian was devastated and could not get the picture of his wife's face out of his mind. He rang the hospice and asked if he could come in and talk about what had happened. After talking through how his wife had died and being reassured by the staff that she had died peacefully he relaxed and was able to begin to bring back other memories and to grieve.

We can also help by giving bereaved people permission to use the time with the dead person as they wish. They will often talk to the dead person, saying things that they did not say when he or she was alive and attempting to conclude unfinished business. Some people may wish to make their own ritual to help them begin to say goodbye. They may wish to read a poem or a prayer, sing, play or listen to music. Again we can help people feel free to be themselves. It helps to make available prayers and readings from religious and non-religious sources.

If the bereaved decide that they do not wish to view the dead person we should respect their wish. Following intra-uterine deaths and the death of newborn babies, it is now routine to take a photograph of the dead baby, and this has been found to be helpful to the parents. The key carer should be told of the existence of these photographs, which they may choose to keep or to leave in the case notes.

Since all of the memories of viewing the body will tend to stay in the person's mind, it is important to make the experience as benign as it can be. The design of a pleasant mortuary chapel with subdued lighting, curtains and flowers, comfortable chairs to sit on and a bed rather than a trolley in which the body can be placed all make for a less traumatic experience than is usual in the clinical setting of a hospital mortuary. A nurse should accompany the family and should normally warn the family that the patient will feel cold, since they may well get a shock if they had not realized that the body will have been refrigerated. The nurse can demonstrate by running a comb through the person's hair that it is all right to touch, then withdraw to allow the family full access. Nurses should remain at hand in case they are needed but should reassure the family that they can stay as long as they wish.

In temperate climates, when deaths occur at home, there is no reason why the body cannot remain at home, in an unheated room, for several days. In the past the funeral commonly left from the home but this is seldom the case today and most people have the body removed to the funeral parlour where it can be refrigerated and viewed on request.

Post-mortem examination

Attitudes to post-mortem examination vary. Most people do not like to think that the body of a loved person is to be subjected to further mutilation, but they may agree to allow it if they are persuaded that some good can come of it. Some Moslems and members of other faiths who believe in the resurrection of the body take strong objection to any such thing and believe that the spirit of the dead person will be harmed.

It follows that in requesting permission for a post-mortem examination the greatest tact is needed and pressure should never be put on those who refuse. In the event that a coroner has ordered a post-mortem the family have no right to refuse and it is the responsibility of the coroner or the coroner's officer to explain the situation. Most coroner's officers take time to support families at this time.

Whatever the circumstances, it is always important to offer to meet a representative of the family after the post-mortem has taken place. They have a right to know what was learned from the examination in broad outline, although most will not want too much detail. This meeting also enables us to assess how they are getting on and how they feel about the post-mortem. It is common for people to wonder if there was anything that they or others could have done to prevent the death and we are usually in a position to reassure them on this issue.

Organ donation

Similar tact is required in requesting organs for transplant. Again there are some people who will object on religious grounds, but others like to think that another sick person has been helped as a consequence of a death that might otherwise have seemed meaningless. The bereaved need to know that the body of the person they love will be treated with respect and they will be less likely to agree to donate if they suspect that the doctor who requests the donation is not respectful. The doctor's role is to explain the need in terms which the family can understand. It is then up to them to decide whether or not they will agree and we should make it clear that they will not be penalized in any way if they refuse.

Since both the identity of the donor and the recipient are confidential and it is likely that some time will need to elapse before the outcome of the donation is known, it is not often possible to inform relatives of the result of the donation. If thanks have been expressed, however, it is important to ensure that they reach the donor family.

Another kind of donation is the offer of bodies for anatomical study. This is, of course, of great value in medical education. It is good practice for teaching hospitals to hold regular memorial services at which the medical students and others who have benefited from the donation can show their respect for the dead people whom they have dissected and meet those family members and friends of the dead person who wish to attend. The students themselves are usually glad to attend and feel that they too have benefited. It is not unreasonable to guess that people who show respect for the dead are also more likely to respect the living.

The first contact after bereavement

If a patient has died in a hospice or hospital the family will normally return to the hospital the following day to collect the death certificate and the patient's belongings. If the patient died at home it is still important for the primary carer to make a visit. This visit provides us with an opportunity to undertake several important things:

- to meet again with the family in order to express our condolences and say goodbye;
- to answer any questions about the patient's death or illness;
- to assess the need for further bereavement counselling.

Contacts from professional carers already known to the bereaved person are usually welcomed during this early phase of grief. Doctors, nurses and social workers who have become trusted confidants provide a tangible link with the dead person, and talking over the events leading up to the death with those who knew what happened helps to make the loss real. Some bereaved people will have questions about treatment or the way in which the patient died, and taking the time to answer these questions can be very beneficial. It can dissipate angry feelings and lessen the likelihood of unnecessary guilt developing. People often keep their thoughts to themselves while the patient is alive; after the death it becomes easier to criticize or question the people in authority. Family members may also want to express their thanks for the care that has been given and seek reassurance that nothing more could or should have been done.

Bereavement risk assessment

If this has not been carried out before bereavement it should be carried out as soon as possible afterwards. The risk factors which need to be considered were described on pages 105–112. They enable us to identify people who will benefit from counselling. In a study by Relf (1986), 30% of families of patients who died in a hospice were assessed as being at risk and were referred to the hospice bereavement service. Similar proportions have been found in other settings (Parkes, 1996).

All things considered, it is not surprising that many people need help from outside the family when they are seriously ill or bereaved. In the chapters which follow we shall examine who should provide that help and how it can be given.

All bereaved people should be given written information about the help that is available to them both locally and nationally. Many people are unduly alarmed because they do not know what to expect. Ideally, this information should be included in a short leaflet which describes the kinds of emotion and other reactions which they are likely to experience in the course of grief.[1] The newly bereaved are unlikely to be ready to assess their need for support soon after the loss and may well turn down an offer which, a few weeks later, they would be glad to accept. If support is to be provided by known professional staff beyond the first weeks of bereavement, the new focus of the relationship will need to be established.

Phase II. Adjustment

Once the funeral is over and the extended social network of family and friends has dispersed, people may begin to take stock. It is at

1   A suitable leaflet has been published by Relf *et al.* (1986).

this time that they often begin to feel the need for bereavement support.

A variety of types of service are likely to be available which may help people to cope with bereavement. It is important for us to be familiar with all of the possible sources of help in a locality and to appraise the strengths and the weaknesses of each if we are to advise bereaved people where they should go for help.

Six types of service are commonly available:

- mental health services,
- self-help (or mutual help) groups,
- befriending services,
- social activities,
- volunteer counselling services,
- group counselling.

These will be described as if they were quite distinct, but in fact there is often a fair amount of overlap between them and some organizations provide more than one of them.

Mental health services

These fall outside the scope of this book (for an account of psychotherapy with the bereaved see Parkes and Sills, 1994). They comprise professional psychiatric and psychological services for the small minority of bereaved people who develop psychiatric disorders following bereavement. As such they provide an important resource for the front line of health care providers and bereavement counsellors and need to foster close working relationships with them. Not only does this facilitate appropriate referrals to these professionals, but it also ensures that the professionals make appropriate use of the counselling and other services available. Many professionals enjoy working in tandem with volunteer bereavement counsellors, who may be asked to continue to provide help to their clients after they have been seen by a professional. Psychiatrists will sometimes prescribe and monitor medication for a patient who may then be better able, with the psychiatrist's approval, to make use of the help of a counsellor.

Professional psychiatrists, psychologists and social workers are often willing to help in the selection, training and supervision of volunteers and may have the knowledge and authority to get an organization started.

In some areas clinical psychologists accept referrals only from psychiatrists, who thereby act as gatekeepers to the psychological services, but they are increasingly accepting referrals from a wider range of health care professionals. The service which they offer to bereaved people varies from one area to another but would typically include help with anxiety management, phobias, panic syndrome, obsessive-compulsive disorders and the full range of stress reactions, including post-traumatic stress disorder and pathological grief reactions. Psychiatrists are trained to help with all of these disorders plus the major psychoses and all of those situations for which drugs are the treatment of choice. Their experience and legal powers make them particularly appropriate sources of help to people who become a risk to themselves or others.

Self-help or mutual help groups

These are run by veterans, people who have themselves experienced the trauma which the group aims to ameliorate. The qualification for offering help is the experience of having been bereaved, and helpers are usually untrained and sometimes unselected. Mutual help groups are usually leaderless, open groups that rely entirely on their members to support each other. Mutual help groups are exemplified by the Compassionate Friends, an organization run by and for parents who have lost a child by death. These organizations may also be able to provide individual help in addition to group support. See Appendix 1 for further particulars about some of these organizations.

An advantage of these organizations is that people who have experienced a trauma expect to be understood by others in similar circumstances. This is of particular importance to people who are or feel stigmatized, such as those bereaved by suicide, but it also applies whenever people have undergone an experience which sets them aside from others. Bereavement by murder is so horrific and frightening an experience that friends and others may back away because they do not know what to do. The bereaved feel alienated from others by the very nature of their bereavement. Parents who have lost a child frequently find that other parents avoid them. By contrast, people who have suffered similar losses know what to say and have no reason to back away. They may even be able to educate each other by sharing what they have learned.

The disadvantages of these organizations are twofold:

(1) Mutual help groups make no distinction between helper and client. This means that there is no way in which helpers can be selected or trained and a standard of care assured.

(2) Experience of similar losses does not guarantee that those who suffer them will understand or know how to help each other. Each person's experience is unique and some may feel that they are being forced into a group identity that does not fit them.

As we have seen, some people react to bereavement by becoming angry; others do not. A mutual help group that has become dominated by angry people will repel those who fear or do not feel anger.

Despite these problems the majority of people who seek help from the organizations listed above feel glad of the help that they get and we should do all in our power to reach out to them and support their work. There is no reason why selected members of mutual help groups should not receive training and support from outside the group and they can then reduce the risks described above.

Befriending

This term has been used to describe types of help falling between ordinary friendship and counselling. Most befriending services make no claims to expertise or offer any help other than friendship and understanding of loss. They are particularly helpful to people who find themselves socially isolated. Many of those who offer befriending have had little or no training and usually work without supervision. There is, therefore, a danger that they will get out of their depth. Organizers of befriending schemes should be aware of this and establish links with other services so that referrals can easily be made.

Social activities

Social activities are common ways of providing support and are offered by many hospices and by most bereavement services. They seek to combat loneliness and the feelings of social isolation commonly experienced by bereaved people.

Social groups have advantages and disadvantages. One way in which people gain support is by comparing themselves with others. This can lead to understanding, recognition and the sense that one is not alone. Unfortunately it can also have the opposite effect. People may compare themselves unfavourably with others and judge themselves harshly. A person whose brother had died felt she had no right to feel so bad and no real right to be at a social meeting after she found herself mainly with people grieving the loss of a spouse.

Timing is important. Social groups can seem daunting in the early months after bereavement. Relf, in an unpublished study, evaluated a series of social meetings at Michael Sobell House aimed at people bereaved three to six months earlier. Many people commented that it was very difficult to listen to other people's stories when they felt so full of their own emotions. Indeed, it seemed that a major reason for coming was to see members of staff whom they had known during the illness. Social groups are most likely to meet bereaved people's needs after the acute period of grief is over. They can then act as a bridge back to the community of non-bereaved people. Run in conjunction with counselling services they can enable bereaved people to graduate from individual counselling to a social group before moving on to other, more daunting, types of socialization. Care must be taken to prevent groups becoming a kind of ghetto for bereaved people and silting up with those who are clinging to a new identity as a 'mourner'. If we allow this we are encouraging the perpetuation of social withdrawal.

Since the main purpose of social groups is to act as a bridge, it is appropriate for most of the activities of the group to be run by the members themselves. Professionals should hold back from leadership roles and should see themselves as facilitating initiatives rather than running the group themselves. This will help prevent counsellors having to devote excessive amounts of time to running social groups.

Volunteer bereavement counselling services

These have been pioneered in the United Kingdom, where there is a tradition of voluntary help. This does not mean that they are not possible in other places and enthusiasts have often disproved the claim 'You won't find people volunteering here'. One of the most exciting lessons that has been learned in hospices and bereavement services across the world is the enormous fund of goodwill that exists towards the dying and the bereaved and which leads people who might not normally consider volunteering to offer their help.

These services are of two types, proactive and reactive. By a *proactive* service we mean one that makes a direct offer of help to people who need the service. Most hospice bereavement services are proactive and many of them use risk assessment as a means of deciding who is in need. A *reactive* service relies on advertising or personal recommendation to inform bereaved people of its existence and leaves it to them to decide whether or not to ask for help. Cruse: Bereavement Care is an example of such a service which has branches in most parts of the United Kingdom. At the time of writing only proactive services have stood the test of scientific evaluation (Raphael, 1986; Parkes, 1981; Relf, 1994). For this reason we prefer proactive services whenever risk assessment is possible but there are, of course, many situations in which this not the case, and reactive services will always be needed.

Parkes' (1981) research indicates that volunteer bereavement counsellors, who have been carefully selected and trained for the job and who carry out their work under supervision, are capable of providing help which is almost as effective in reducing stress symptoms and the consumption of drugs, alcohol and tobacco, as that provided by an experienced psychiatrist. In addition Relf (1994) has shown that the use of such services reduces the use made by bereaved people of health care services, particularly from GPs. Volunteers are less likely than health care professionals to stigmatize clients or to encourage them to think of grief as an illness.

Bereavement services, such as those offered at Sir Michael Sobell House and by Cruse, expect their counsellors to undergo stringent selection procedures aimed at finding out how committed they are, how they have coped with losses in the past and what current stresses exist in their lives. People who have been bereaved for less than two years are not accepted. All must complete a minimum of 60 hours of training which aims to help volunteers to draw on their personal experience, to listen to other people's experiences, to learn appropriate theory, to develop and practise ways of working with clients and to practise communication and relationship-building skills. A variety of training methods may be used. Experiential exercises (including role play) and self-exploration are the most important of these. Volunteers should complete a period of service under close supervision before they become fully accredited by the organization. Much of the supervision and training is given by professionals who are a part of the service and available to take over if the need arises.

It is often possible to match the counsellor to the client and this is particularly important if the problems are complex (when an experienced counsellor or professional may be needed) or the client has strong preferences for a particular age, sex, ethnicity or religion. It is wise to recruit counsellors from all of the ethnic and religious groups likely to be found in the client population.

Members of the health care professions also benefit from the kind of training described above and organizations such as Cruse and some hospices provide courses aimed at professionals. Cruse also publishes a wide range of low-cost literature for counsellors, including the international journal *Bereavement Care*. *Lifeline* is the newsletter of the National Association of Bereavement Services.

Group counselling

Group counselling requires people to leave their homes and meet with others who are initially strangers and whom the bereaved person has no reason to trust. Because members of the group are all bereaved they are likely to talk about bereavement and this in itself can deter people who are shy, fearful of expressing emotion or of 'breaking down'. It follows that groups are seldom acceptable to people in the early stages of grieving.

The great strength of group counselling is the opportunity that it presents for people who are in the same life situation to learn from each other. This means that groups will work best when their members share certain things in common. Widows with young or school-aged children, widowers, adults who have lost a parent, homosexuals who have lost a partner, people bereaved by suicide, parents who have lost a child or old people whose spouse has died – people in each of these categories have a great deal to learn from others who fall into the same category. They have less to learn from heterogeneous groups and will probably drop out if they feel that their special problems have not been understood. It follows that it is easier to organize such groups in large urban centres which contain sufficient numbers of people in these categories to make it possible to set up viable groups.

Unlike the groups for cancer patients which were described in Chapter 4, groups for bereaved people are less likely to dwindle in size and can, therefore, be organized as either closed or open groups. The ideal number is 8–12 group members but, in order to ensure that this number will attend, it may be necessary to recruit about 20 for each group. With more than 12 it is hard for everyone to be heard and with less than 8 some of the advantages of pooling knowledge and support are lost. Members of very small groups often feel under pressure to attend in order to maintain the group and become self-conscious in their efforts to make the group work.

Closed groups expect all members to attend for a fixed number of group meetings. This gives the group members more time to learn to trust each other and this, in turn, makes it easier for them to share feelings and secrets. It also enables the organizers to hold a series of groups to meet different types of special problem.

Open groups, on the other hand, appeal to people who do not wish to commit themselves to regular attendance and prefer to 'drop in'. They tend to be set up on a long-term basis and to take place less frequently than closed groups. There is, however, a danger that open groups will become dominated by a core or clique of long-term members who will eventually make it difficult to admit new members, and discourage those who do attend. For this reason it is advisable for these groups to be ended every year or so. Typically a closed group will be set up to meet once a week for six to ten weeks while an open group will take place once a month and run for up to a year.

For further details on group counselling, see Cruse (1995).

Bereavement Counselling

Bereavement counselling involves the use of the counselling skills described in Chapter 3 with the specific aim of enabling bereaved people to work through their grief and come to an understanding of their experience of loss. It aims to facilitate normal grief by:

- establishing a supportive relationship;
- helping bereaved people identify and express their feelings;
- reassuring them of the normality of common grief experiences;
- assisting with problem solving;
- providing continuing and reliable support.

Establishing a supportive relationship. Bereavement counselling relies on developing a warm and trusting relationship between the helper and client. This involves using all the counselling skills described in Chapter 3. We need to listen with our total attention, to respond in a way that demonstrates our willingness to enter their world and to be non-judgemental, calm and steady despite the client's depth of anguish.

Helping the bereaved person identify and express feelings. Bereaved people experience powerful feelings such as anger, guilt, anxiety, helplessness and despair, which may be difficult to express with family and friends. Support can enable clients to express and explore their feelings and help them to feel less out of control of their emotions. It is important to respect the client's pace and to identify what he or she is experiencing. Some people find it very hard to find the language to describe what they are feeling: they just hurt. Working with problematic feelings will be described later in this chapter.

Reassuring people of the normality of grief. There is little understanding of grief in modern developed societies and many people are unduly worried by common reactions such as the illusion of seeing or hearing the dead person. It is important to say that what is being experienced is natural for someone who has been bereaved. However, care must be taken when offering such reassurance. If reassurance is given too soon the client may feel that worries are simply being dismissed.

Assisting with problem solving. One of the tasks of grieving is adjusting to life without the person who has died (Worden, 1982). The deceased will have played many roles and fulfilled many functions in the bereaved person's life. Many people feel daunted by the immensity of their loss and lack confidence in their ability to find solutions to what can appear to be insurmountable problems. Bereavement support involves helping clients think through how they will manage the changes arising from their loss. It should facilitate decision making and problem solving. Helping people identify their resources and manage their difficulties restores feelings of self-esteem.

Providing continuing and reliable support. Knowing that bereavement support is regularly available for a time promotes feelings of self-worth. Bereaved people frequently find that, after the first weeks of mourning have passed, few people are willing to listen. This causes them to feel that their loss and what they are experiencing is no longer of interest and causes them to feel isolated and dislocated from others. The willingness of the counsellor to carry on listening and to provide reliable support counters these feelings and encourages a sense of safety at a time of insecurity.

Letting Go and Moving Forwards

In all of this work we need to bear in mind the normal course of grief, and Worden's tasks of grieving provide a useful frame of reference (these were described on pages 15–17). We showed there that grieving requires us to let go of certain aspects of the past and move forwards. To *let go* we have to:

* accept the reality of the loss;
* work through the pain of grief.

To *move forwards* we have to:

* adjust to a world in which the lost person is missing;
* build on those aspects of the past relationship that remain important to us; in other words, to relocate the deceased.

This is what is meant by the work of grieving. It takes time and cannot be hurried. Nor does it help much to explain it to people. People who have not yet begun to accept the need to let go may well resent the suggestion that this is what they must do and they will certainly not be ready to think about moving forwards. We must not try to force the pace by making them fit into our model. The concept of tasks of grieving is, therefore, no more useful to the bereaved person than the concept of stages of grief. They are, however, useful to the counsellor in providing us with a frame of reference, a way of thinking about the progress that is being made, or not being made. They enable us to recognize and encourage movement and to identify problems that may be holding up the process of grieving.

Getting Started

Acceptability

If an offer of help to a bereaved person is to be accepted it needs to have credibility. Many people are understandably suspicious of any stranger who comes into their home at a time when they are feeling vulnerable and it is not surprising that many offers of help to the bereaved are rejected. The situation is much easier if someone known to the bereaved person is able to recommend the service, and the service is sponsored by a trusted organization. Printed information about the service, outlining its objectives and policies, including confidentiality and the selection, training and supervision of volunteers, should be provided. This should be followed up by a telephone call from a counsellor who is not too 'pushy'. It is important to reassure people that what you discuss will be treated as confidential but to explain that you do receive guidance and support.

Location

Because most people feel secure in their own homes this is often the best place in which to provide counselling. On the other hand, interruptions are common, particularly if there are small children at home, and some clients prefer to be seen in the privacy of an office. Unless the client is known by the team to be trustworthy it is not advisable to send a female counsellor alone into the home of a male client. Such clients are better seen in an office where others are to hand or, if this is not possible, the counsellor should be accompanied.

Timing

Usually family and friends rally round to provide support and practical help during the early weeks of bereavement and it can be hard for bereaved people to assess whether or not they want ongoing help. If there is thought to be an urgent need for help at this time, perhaps because of a suspicion that there may be a risk of suicide or mental illness, then it may be more appropriate for this risk to be assessed by a mental health professional rather than a counsellor. If, however, that help is refused, or people who are not in urgent need are asking for help, then we should not hesitate to invite a counsellor to make an early visit. If the need is less urgent most hospice-based services wait four to eight weeks before making contact.

Negotiating the framework for care

Whether care is to be provided within the context of an existing relationship or by someone previously unknown, it is important to work out clearly with the bereaved person what is being agreed. The idea of negotiating the purpose and the limits of involvement may seem difficult, but it is necessary to discuss what you are in a position to offer so that the bereaved can decide whether or not this is what they want and know what to expect from the relationship. Providing information enables power to be shared.

Few people do, in fact, know what to expect from bereavement counselling or support. Relf's study of a hospice bereavement service found that most people welcomed contact but some were at first uncertain about *how* to use support (Relf, 1994). People may be reassured to hear that others have found that talking to someone from outside their social network is helpful because they have found it hard to talk about feelings to close family and friends. It is important to say roughly how long each session will last, the likely frequency of contact and that, while the length of involvement will be guided by how useful they are finding the support, it will be time limited. It helps to say that some people want support for a year or more, but others find that just a few visits are all that is required. Suggesting that you review your involvement after four or five meetings is very useful. This helps people who are uncertain to accept help knowing that they have a legitimate opportunity to end the relationship if it is proving unsatisfactory. It also provides sufficient time for trust to develop and demonstrates our belief in their ability to make decisions at a time when they may be feeling out of control of much of their lives.

It is, of course, inappropriate to start discussing the purpose and limits of bereavement counselling with people who are over-whelmed with emotion. If this is the case, negotiating what they can expect from the relationship should be postponed until they are able to participate. It is, however, important to discuss these issues as early as possible in the relationship, otherwise an expectation of perpetual support can arise and make it difficult to end involvement satisfactorily.

Counsellors may be understandably apprehensive that an offer of support will be misunderstood, particularly when the client is of the opposite sex. The loss of the physical relationship with a spouse or partner may cause some bereaved people to misconstrue warmth and concern as an invitation to further intimacy. The counsellor may become aware of this misunderstanding in various ways: a hug that feels too close, personal remarks or compliments or invitations to the counsellor to take part in social events. The training of counsellors should include a session on helping them to understand how to minimize misunderstandings and how to react in a way that, while preserving personal safety, does not cause the counsellor to belittle the client. If the counsellor is a volunteer it is particularly important to make it perfectly clear that this is a relationship which is governed by the same rules as those applying to relationships with doctors and other professional caregivers.

Moira, a volunteer in her early 30s working with a bereavement service, was visiting Harry, a widower aged 70. Harry had experienced very few relationships with women that did not contain a strong sexual element and began to 'woo' Moira by having food and wine ready for her when she visited and by inviting her to accompany him to the theatre. Moira, through supervision, was able to recognize that he was trying to understand the nature and boundaries of this new type of relationship. She explained that he did not need to give her food or invitations in order to maintain her support and recognized his vulnerability. Harry realized that Moira was not interested in an intimate relationship and, as his trust developed, he began to express his regret and guilt over his numerous extramarital affairs and the effect they had on his wife. Moira did not judge his behaviour but continued to support him through the first year after his loss.

In this example Moira maintained a professional relationship in several ways. She did not hide the fact that she was married, but did not divulge intimate details about her private life. She was careful to ensure that her body language was congruent with what she was saying and she gave no opportunities for Harry to touch her. She did not show fear or revulsion at his advances. Moira's acceptance freed Harry and enabled him to get in touch with his underlying pain and eventually come to terms with his guilt. Had Moira felt that she was in physical danger she would have had no doubts about withdrawing.

Refusals

It is not always possible to establish a relationship. Bereaved people may find that it is simply too painful to dwell on their loss, or find the idea of talking about their feelings too difficult to contemplate. Some may simply not get on with their supporter. While it is not advisable to force our attentions on bereaved people who do not want our help, we should not assume that this means that they will always feel the same. If we have grounds for thinking that they are at risk, a follow-up call a month or two later will give them a chance to change their mind, and it demonstrates that we have not forgotten them. We also need to make sure that they know how to make contact with us or with anyone else who might be acceptable to them. Some people will accept help from a woman while they would refuse a man, some from a black person but not a white, some from a counsellor but not a psychiatrist. We all have our fears and our prejudices. Our aim must be to recognize the client's point of view and work within it. If that means that someone whom we believe to be in need of our help does not get it, then so be it. No system of care is perfect and there are some people who cannot be helped by counselling.

Ongoing Counselling

Once trust has been established the relationship enters a new phase. Their increased sense of security enables most bereaved people to share their feelings more freely and explore the consequences of their loss. Their informed and empathic understanding of the situation enables counsellors to accompany the bereaved person in their loss. Sessions may include looking at photographs and sharing memories as aspects of the lost relationship are explored and placed in perspective. Strong feelings, including anger, despair, extreme sorrow and guilt, may be expressed and the bereaved may become very anxious and fearful. Some experience disturbing physical symptoms; they may question their beliefs and find that previous certainties have deserted them.

An important part of this phase of counselling is assessing progress. Usually this will be steady, with minor setbacks, but there is great variation from one person to another. It is important to take a reasonably long-term perspective. Thus, it is common for bereaved people to 'bump along on the bottom' (as one counsellor put it) for some time, feeling sad, lonely and unable to look to the future; they may go over the same problems again and again. In such circumstances counsellors may feel that no progress is being made and may be tempted to withdraw prematurely. It is very hard for inexperienced counsellors to believe that grieving is a process that will take time rather than a state that will go on for ever.

Keeping accurate records is a great help because it enables us to look back over time and to recognize the progress that *is* being made. Sharing this with the bereaved can do much to bolster their self-esteem. If, on the other hand, it is clear that no progress is being made we may justly suspect that the grief is becoming complicated. Bereavement may reawaken old problems or exacerbate pre-existing tensions with family or friends. Memories of past traumas may be reawakened, particularly if the bereaved was subjected to abuse by a partner or parent. Faced with these problems some people become clinically depressed. Bereavement counsellors need to know enough about such problems to recognize them when they are present, but they should not be expected to have the expertise to treat them and it is important that they know when to ask for help and from whom.

The Dimensions of Loss

Susan LePoidevin's 'dimensions of loss' constitute a useful checklist of the seven areas to which we need to pay attention in counselling the bereaved. They constitute a practical tool which enables us to examine systematically each of the main ways in which bereavement influences the human mind, body and social network, and to remind ourselves what problems and resources can be brought to bear. Although widely used by counsellors who attended LePoidevin's training courses on bereavement, these remained unpublished at her untimely death in 1989. Each of them is a dimension which is bound to be affected by bereavement. If, in the course of an interview, they are not all covered spontaneously, it is worth asking a few additional questions to check how the client is coping in each dimension. Similarly it is useful, when keeping case records and reporting to a supervisor or team, to note any changes in each dimension. Over time this enables us to build up an accurate picture of the individual's response to loss.

The dimensions are:

- identity;
- physical;
- emotional;
- family/community;
- lifestyle;
- practical;
- spiritual.

Identity includes the ways in which bereavement affects our inner world – the way we think about ourselves and our capabilities.

The *physical* dimension includes stress-related symptoms as described on page 14, as well as minor illnesses reflecting loss of resilience. It is not uncommon for bereaved people to imagine that they are suffering from symptoms similar to those suffered by the person who has died. Whatever the cause of these symptoms, the more people worry about them the worse they tend to get. It is always wise to ask clients about their health if this has not been discussed in the course of a meeting.

Emotional components may be expressed or hidden. Men are particularly likely to conceal their feelings. This may have an important influence on their sense of wellbeing and may cause great concern if the feelings break through, or give rise to psychosomatic problems if they are repressed. Although it is unwise to try to force people to express feelings that are being repressed, a simple question – 'How do you feel about that?' – will often give people the permission they need to acknowledge the existence of feelings.

Family and community are important influences and may themselves be affected by the bereavement. Counsellors should find out how the family are responding to the loss and whether such responses are helpful or unhelpful, what support is the client receiving from or giving to others, and what new roles the client is taking on.

Lifestyle is often affected by the loss. The counsellor needs to know how the client's financial status, housing and occupational prospects have been affected.

The *practical* dimension includes the bereaved person's ability to cope with the demands of everyday living, looking after children or other dependants, getting to work and so on.

The *spiritual* dimension is essentially concerned with finding meaning in life. It is important for the counsellor to understand how bereavement has affected the bereaved person's beliefs about the world, faith and spiritual 'core'.

It is useful to check each of these dimensions when writing reports on counselling.

Ending

Ending relationships always involves feelings of loss. When working with a bereaved person the way in which the intervention is brought to a close is particularly important because it may resonate with the original loss. Feelings associated with that bereavement may come to the surface and this element of reflected loss can make it difficult to withdraw. It is important to remember that ending is different and that it may provide clients with an opportunity to learn by experiencing loss in a situation they can influence to a degree that was not possible with the original loss. Endings need to be well prepared; indeed, it is important to plan the ending from the beginning.

We have already discussed the importance of establishing boundaries in the early days of involvement. One of the reasons for doing this is that it prepares the ground for the eventual closure. Making it clear from the beginning that it is unlikely that help will be needed in the long term conveys the helper's belief in the bereaved person's capacity to survive. This subtly promotes self-esteem and hope for the future. It makes it possible to refer to the eventual ending and provides a context for reviewing progress.

If the ending is not mentioned, difficulties may arise for both parties. As the relationship develops the bereaved person may find it hard to imagine that there will come a time when he or she will not need support. This is a natural part of bereavement work, but if clients become too dependent they will both have failed. This is much more likely to happen if no guidance about the usual length of involvement has been given. We have found that inexperienced bereavement supporters find it particularly difficult to prepare for closure. Their concerns focus on being accepted by the bereaved person and establishing trust and it can feel dangerous to introduce anything that may threaten that trust.

Usually bereaved people indicate when the time to close is approaching. Feelings will be experienced as less overwhelming and there will be a sense of being able to manage the low times; perhaps there will have been a turning point or a breakthrough. It helps to prepare for the ending by acknowledging the bereaved person's progress and by increasing the interval between sessions.

A Case Study

Amy died of a rare abdominal cancer. Her partner, Jeremy (33), was left to raise three children: Ann (8), Amy's daughter by a previous marriage, Stephan (2) and Kate (1) (see Fig. 6.1). Jeremy was a social worker. He refused formal support in his place of work for fear that exposing his vulnerability might affect his career

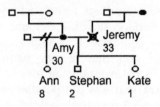

Figure 6.1 Genogram of Jeremy's family.

prospects. However, he willingly accepted the support of a volunteer counsellor attached to the hospice in which his wife had died.

Getting started. The volunteer, Judy, telephoned Jeremy five weeks after Amy's death. She told Jeremy who she was and what the service could offer. She did not invite Jeremy to tell his story over the telephone but restricted herself to being clear about the arrangements and warm in manner. Jeremy opted to see her at the hospice because he feared that it would be impossible to talk at home without interruptions. Judy closed the conversation by repeating her name and ensuring that Jeremy had the telephone number of the bereavement service so that he could contact her.

At the *first meeting* Judy introduced herself and explained her role. Jeremy asked about confidentiality and was reassured to learn that Judy would not refer to him by name in discussing his case in supervision meetings. In the first meeting Jeremy talked solely about his children's needs and behaviour (*practical and lifestyle dimensions*). Towards the end of this meeting Judy felt that a good basis for counselling had been established. She suggested that they meet for an hour, once a fortnight to begin with, and that they review progress and decide upon future counselling after six meetings. Jeremy agreed to this plan and seemed reassured to know what to expect.

The second meeting followed the pattern of the first, with Jeremy spending most of the time talking about the children. Towards the end of this meeting Judy suggested that Jeremy tell her about how his wife's death was affecting him. With this encouragement he was able to spend time talking about Amy's illness, the delay in diagnosis and his own guilt at not recognizing its seriousness. He expressed much anger against his GP and recognized that this was preventing him from taking his children to the surgery (*emotional dimension*). At this session it was clear that trust had been established. Jeremy subsequently had a very honest exchange of views with his GP which ended with the GP expressing his sadness at Amy's death and inviting Jeremy to seek him out at any time.

Session three began with Jeremy recalling, with admiration, how Amy had responded to the news that she was going to die. That evening she had been furious and shouted, 'I won't be a heroine'; she had then thrown a pan full of Brussels sprouts at Jeremy. Recalling this event Jeremy began to weep. He acknowledged, for the first time, that he did not know how he was going to bring up the children on his own.

This session was a turning point. Subsequently Jeremy began to look at other sources of help, remembering that his parents-in-law had offered to take the children at weekends and that his own father had also offered to help. He realized that he was under no obligation to do everything himself and explored with Judy how he could share the load without letting Amy or the children down (*social network, lifestyle*).

In the next two sessions Jeremy explored his feelings of abandonment. He recalled how he had felt as a child when his parents had sent him to a boarding school while they were living in India. He had felt like an outsider and was bitter with his parents for ignoring his pleas for them to return home. Judy suggested that he now felt as if he were in the foreign country of the single parent without knowing the customs or the language (*identity and lifestyle*). Once this had been established Jeremy indicated that he would value the opportunity to talk and read about grieving children, because he did not want his own children to feel abandoned. He realized that he had always relied on Amy to make sense of the children's feelings and behaviour. Was it normal for eight-year-old Ann to creep into his bed at night? He understood her feelings because of his own experience, but he also recognized the fact that he was not her true father and worried that this behaviour might be interpreted as incestuous. As a social worker he was only too aware of the risks. He was reassured to learn that many bereaved children sought this type of comfort, which usually stopped of its own accord. It need not be a problem for her unless it was a problem for him. Jeremy laughed; she was certainly in no danger from him.

Jeremy also sought information about the experience of bereavement in babyhood. He was very sad to think that Stephan and Kate would not remember their mother as the person she was. Judy encouraged him to put together a 'memory box' of photographs and treasured possessions that might help them to remember and deepen their knowledge of Amy.

As agreed, Jeremy and Judy reviewed progress at the *sixth session* and agreed to continue meeting until after the first anniversary of Amy's death but to gradually increase the gaps between meetings. Jeremy said that he greatly valued the meetings and wanted them to continue. He recognized that Judy seldom came up with solutions to his problems but he trusted her and felt that her attentiveness reassured him that he was valuable.

At subsequent meetings Jeremy felt able to explore his feelings of sexual and emotional loneliness. This seemed to make it easier for him to talk about a new casual relationship and to acknowledge the continuing feelings of guilt and dissatisfaction that then arose.

Eight months after Amy's death the headstone for her grave was erected. It simply stated Amy's name and the dates of her birth and death. Amy's parents had wanted a more pious inscription but Jeremy had objected (*social*). As he recounted the conflict he suddenly exploded with rage at the God whom he had believed in as a child. 'How can I tell the children that God loves them when he robs them of their mother?' he shouted (*spiritual*). Judy listened without comment, knowing that only Jeremy could find new meaning for his life after the apparently senseless tragedy of Amy's death.

As the first anniversary approached, Jeremy began to review the year. He recognized that he had come a long way; he had established routines of practical care, returned to full-time work and was being well supported by his colleagues, who allowed him time off when crises arose. He no longer felt that he had to find another partner if he was to survive but was not closing the door to the possibility that one might come along. He acknowledged, with some surprise, that he was enjoying being a parent and that he was now feeling physically well for the first time for many months. His step-daughter, Ann, had been experiencing stomach cramps and Jeremy wondered if these were related to the similar symptoms suffered by her mother. Judy agreed that it was not uncommon for children to develop symptoms resembling the illness of a dead parent but advised Jeremy to take her for a checkup to the doctor (*physical*).

Two extra sessions were needed following an event in which Ann and some friends had dressed up in Amy's clothes and Amy's wedding ring had been lost down the drain. Jeremy had lost his temper and hit Ann. Subsequently he was shaken by the intensity of his feelings and needed the extra time to re-establish confidence in himself.

Despite this, *the final session* was a time for celebration. Both Jeremy and Judy felt that a lot had been achieved and were pleased with the outcome of counselling. Judy acknowledged to her supervisor that this case had triggered in her feelings that she had experienced after her divorce when she too had had to struggle to bring up her children as a single parent. She had found supervision very helpful in enabling her to disentangle her own from Jeremy's needs and to continue to focus on Jeremy's needs.

Family Counselling after Bereavement

Family counselling is a relatively new area in which few people have much experience. We think that it is important and will become more so in the future. Since there are few centres with the resources to give proper training in this field we shall not discuss it in depth here. Those who are fortunate to have training available are recommended to make use of it.

Assuming that an experienced family counsellor is available, the decision whether to counsel one person alone or to counsel more than one member of the same family must depend on the answers to three questions:

(1) Is there a family problem?
(2) If so, will it be more easily dealt with by joint or family interviews than by counselling the individuals separately?
(3) Are the relevant family members willing to accept joint counselling?

If the answer to any of these questions is 'No' then it is better to offer individual help.

By a 'family problem' we mean a problem involving more than one member of a family and disrupting the traditional ways of coping that have become established in this family. It might be thought that all bereavements are 'family problems' but in fact the main burden of bereavement often falls on one person alone and the family may continue to function perfectly well without help and without any need for a change in its traditional ways of coping.

Family problems are likely to arise when a family leader dies, when more than one person has had a problematic relationship with the dead person, when the death is untimely, or when it is a child or young person who has died. In all these cases the ramifications may be extensive and a family approach should be considered.

Joint meetings have the advantage that the family bring the problems into the room with them. It is possible to see the family in action, to assess how they are coping, what patterns of mutual support or defence they adopt and what the consequences are for each member. Family myths become clear and the counsellor becomes aware of any dysfunctional influences that may exist and which may otherwise undermine attempts to help.

A disadvantage of family meetings arises from the tendency of family members to conceal information from each other, either in order to protect each other or because they fear that others will use the information against them. People may try to protect children or other dependants by concealing feelings of grief or anger, by denying problems that exist or by misrepresenting the facts of the situation in order to preserve a family myth.

In such circumstances it is reasonable to offer a mixture of individual and family meetings aimed at providing people with the opportunity to tackle family problems while also meeting their own needs for individual support.

The Bereaved Child

The care of the bereaved child is complex and it is not possible here to do more than touch on some of the major issues. For a more comprehensive coverage of this important field the reader is referred to Grollman (1967), Couldrick (1989), Dyregrov (1991) and Smith and Pennells (1995).

Ideally, all parents should prepare their children for loss, be it that of a pet or a family member; sadly, few do. This neglect stems not out of cruelty, but from a feeling that the kindest way of treating children is to keep them in ignorance of the dark side of life for as long as possible. If, contrary to expectation, a family member should die, the surviving relatives continue this policy by telling the child as little as possible, disguising the facts in pseudo-religious fairy stories (such as 'Daddy is a star in the sky'), and failing to invite them to funerals or other potentially supportive rituals.

Even those parents who would like to be more open with their children find this very difficult. Their own feelings of grief make it difficult for them to talk at all about what has happened and they fear that, if they do, they will break down in front of the children and make things very much worse for them. At the same time, they do not trust anyone else to do it for them.

Children can grieve as soon as they are old enough to become attached, that is, within the first year of life. If deprived of emotional support, their grief will be worse and may lead to lasting difficulties. As they get old enough to understand the difference between temporary and permanent loss, children also need information. This will help them to make sense of their loss; without it they will develop their own explanations for what has happened. These explanations are commonly gross distortions of the truth: 'Daddy has gone to be with Jesus because I was a naughty boy,' or 'Mummy is still in the hospital and will soon be coming home'. These distortions can cause serious problems but are not difficult to correct if the parents become aware of them.

Given the harm that can result from such misunderstandings, it is tempting for counsellors to attempt to take over and fulfil the parental role themselves. This is a mistake – all parents carry the final responsibility for the care of their children and, while we are free to advise them, we have no right to over-rule them, whatever our own views may be. In the end, our main role is to support the parents in the hope that they will come to trust us enough to take our advice on matters of this kind.

The first reaction of children to the death of a parent or sibling is commonly to fear for their own death. 'Who will look after me?' they say, and are surprised when adults see such questions as silly or selfish.

Parents who have suffered a major loss are not only in great need of personal support, they are also waiting for the next disaster. Their own need for succour may cause them to seek support from their own children, and even quite young children are often told that they must now 'Look after mummy'. At the same time, the parent's loss of security may cause him or her to be over-anxious and over-protective of the children. Hence, the children get simultaneous messages that the world is a very dangerous place in which they may not survive, and that they must now grow up and look after their bereaved parent. Small wonder that the children themselves become anxious, bewildered and pettish. Anxiety often triggers bad behaviour which is either ignored (out of pity for the child) or punished (which aggravates the child's feeling of rejection). Either way the child's need for emotional support is not met.

Parents' fears that talking about death to children and involving them in the rituals of funerals and viewing the dead will harm them are seldom justified in reality. Provided that children are properly prepared and supported, they can cope with these and will usually benefit from them in much the same way as adults. Any dangers that exist from inflicting trauma on the children are more than balanced by the dangers of excluding them. It follows that parents should be advised to include their children in such activities and to communicate with them in whatever way is most appropriate to their maturity. For younger children, this may mean initiating or joining in games about death, for play is the way in which children learn about life.

Summary

❏   In the immediate period following a death, support most often needs to be given by the same people who have looked after the patient and family before death. Health care staff should give close support and monitor the needs of families at the time of a patient's death.

❏   Family members should be encouraged to ask questions and be given appropriate explanation and, usually, reassurance about the way the patient has died and the care that was given, particularly if they were not present at the time of death.

❏   It is important to meet the religious and cultural needs of families at this time.

❏   Most people are helped, but some are harmed, by viewing the dead. Staff must assess the risks and help the family to make an informed choice. When family members choose to view the body we must sensitively prepare them and minimize the risk of unpleasant surprises.

❏   The visit by the family on the day after death is an opportunity to express condolences, answer questions and assess the need for further help.

❏   Written information describing grief and giving the addresses of local resources should be given to all bereaved people.

❏   Services that are commonly available include mental health services, self-help (or mutual help) groups, befriending services, social activities, volunteer counselling services and group counselling.

❏   Few services have been properly evaluated at this time and only proactive counselling services reaching out to high-risk bereaved people have been shown to be effective.

❏   The purpose, way of working and likely time scale of counselling should be explained early on.

❏   Accurate records help counsellors to assess progress. This is usually reassuring to counsellor and client.

❏   Counsellors must recognize the limits of their own ability to help and be prepared to refer to others those whom they cannot help.

❏   Dimensions to which attention needs to be paid in the course of counselling include identity, physical, emotional, family and community, lifestyle, practical and spiritual.

❏   The ending of counselling is often another form of bereavement and needs to be prepared for and handled with sensitivity.

❏   Parents and others commonly fail to meet the needs of children for information and support in bereavement. Even so, parents have final responsibility for the care of their children and we have no right to overrule them, whatever our own views may be.

❏   Children can cope with funerals, viewing a dead person and most other situations likely to arise after bereavement, provided they are supported emotionally, given opportunities to talk it through and warned what to expect.

7

Problems in Counselling the Bereaved

In this chapter we shall examine some of the commoner problems that are likely to come to the notice of those who support or counsel the bereaved. In general they can be classed as problems in expressing grief and problems in stopping grieving and getting on with life.

Much has been written by psychoanalysts about the dangers of repressing thoughts and feelings, consigning them to the unconscious mind where they remain, like bombs, waiting to explode in the form of psychotic or neurotic symptoms. This attractive and fashionable explanation for mental illness has had a long run, but evidence for its validity is limited and while it may account for some delayed reactions it certainly does not provide an adequate explanation for more than a small proportion of the problems that follow bereavement.

While there is plenty of evidence that bereaved people often attempt to avoid painful reminders of their loss, and may even cling to unrealistic fantasies that the dead person is still alive, these are not unconscious acts – they are carried out in clear consciousness that the death has, in fact, taken place. People who choose not to visit the cemetery are perfectly aware that the dead body of a loved person is lying there – they are simply choosing not to think about that fact at the present time.

At any given moment we have a hierarchy of demands upon our time and attention. The urge to cry aloud and to search for a lost person often comes high up in that hierarchy but nobody can grieve *all* the time. Before long we must dry our tears and get on with the normal routines of life: eating, sleeping, answering the telephone, doing the shopping. These activities do not mean very much in themselves, and they are certainly not more important than grief, but they necessarily occupy much of the time of bereaved people and may even provide them with temporary distraction from the pangs of grief. There is nothing wrong with that: everybody does it and it does not seriously interfere with the work of grieving.

Furthermore, the majority of those who require psychiatric help after bereavement are not suffering from the effects of repressing grief. More often they are suffering from an inability to stop grieving and get on with living the rest of their lives. Follow-up studies of widows do not indicate that those who grieve most intensely in the first weeks do better than those who do not; on the contrary, they do worse (Parkes and Weiss, 1983).

So, the simplistic assumption that all that the bereaved need to do is grieve does not hold water. On the other hand, neither does the opposite assumption, that people do not need to grieve at all. In the end it appears that what people need is to strike a balance between the expression and the inhibition of grief; too much or too little can cause problems (Stroebe *et al.* in 1994 called this the 'dual process model' of grieving).

Inhibited Grief and its Management

The inhibition and avoidance of grief cause problems only if they go on most of the time, preventing people from facing up to the implications of their loss and postponing pain. When faced with someone who has suffered a bereavement but who is patently not grieving at any time or to any degree we should consider whether something has gone wrong. Sometimes nothing has gone wrong: grief may be absent because the relationship with the lost person was not close or because grieving was completed before the death (for example when the illness caused a personality change or when someone has been seriously ill for a great length of time). Some people have a religious faith that enables them to see all separations as temporary and a secure self-confidence that helps them to tolerate the temporary separation. This is most commonly found in the elderly, who may already be withdrawing from this world and waiting patiently for the next.

But there is a minority whose attempts to avoid the pain of grieving is unsuccessful. They fill their lives with activities, struggle to distract themselves from thoughts they cannot bear, hide away photographs and other reminders of the dead person, and forbid their families from mentioning them by name, and they may even drink themselves into oblivion as a way of getting to sleep at night. But 'grief will out' and nightmares in which the dead person has returned, episodes of unaccountable depression, panic attacks, tearful episodes in public places or worrying physical symptoms which sometimes bear a resemblance to the symptoms suffered by the person who has died – any of these can arise and create a fresh crop of problems for the bereaved who think that they can escape from grief.

Harriet (33) had nursed her husband, Mark, through a series of cerebral haemorrhages which had caused frequent headaches and changed him from a 'gentle giant' to a violent and bad-tempered man. His death, when it came, had been a relief and Harriet had dealt with it by putting it out of her mind and keeping busy. She had exerted a rigid control over her emotions and smoked a great deal. Everyone said how well she had coped. Two years later she met Bill, a divorcee, with whom she was soon cohabiting in a happy relationship.

Just when things were going right for her, three years after Mark's death, Harriet began to suffer from pains behind her ears that strongly resembled the headaches from which he had suffered, so much so that she began to think that she too might die of a stroke. The worse her headaches became, the more frightened she became, and the more frightened, the worse the headaches. By the time she asked for help from her GP she was suffering panic attacks in addition to the headaches.

The counsellor to whom Harriet was referred found her to be a sensitive and intelligent woman who responded positively to his suggestion that her head pains reflected some unfinished business remaining from her spoiled relationship with Mark. For the first time she was able to share her grief at the loss of the man she had loved, her guilt at the anger which his aggressive behaviour had evoked and at the relief which she had felt at his death. She brought pictures of him to the sessions and cried as she apologized to him for what she saw as her failure to go on loving him to the end.

In addition to the counselling she received, she was taught relaxation techniques and given positive explanations and re-assurance about her panic attacks. She soon began to improve and stopped smoking altogether. After only four sessions she was symptom free and in no need of further help.

From the point of view of the counsellor these cases provide an opportunity for dramatically effective results. It is never too late to grieve, and bereaved people who finally decide to share their grief to the full, to 'do the grief work' as Freud would put it, may experience a rapid improvement in their symptoms. Cases of this kind are so rewarding for the client and counsellor that they may tempt us to put pressure on other clients to do the same. 'You *must* cry' can become a torment to the bereaved who cannot cry, either because they do not need to or because they do not yet feel safe enough to do so. We must recognize that people usually have good reasons for doing what they do. People who never cry may have learned early in life that crying is always punished, or they may have discovered other ways to express grief, as laughter or by talking. Either way, we must respect their ways of coping and try to provide a setting in which they can make the best possible use of these.

Many of those who avoid grief will also avoid counselling. If they expect that our aim is to make them 'break down', then we become a symbol of everything they most fear. Clearly, we shall not succeed in helping unless we make it perfectly clear that it is they who set the agenda, not us. Our aim is to make life safer for them, not more unsafe, and we shall not succeed by suggesting that, unless they grieve our way, they will suffer dire consequences. This does not, of course, mean that we have to see the world only through the eyes of the client or agree with points of view which differ from our own. We simply need to respect the right to differ and hope that, if we can open ourselves to the possibility of different ways of viewing the world, the client may do the same.

Some clients will try to put pressure on us to help them to avoid grieving. The commonest way to do this is by means of sedatives and tranquillizers. 'You *must* give me something to make me sleep' is a cry for help that doctors find difficult to resist. Yet sedatives (including the most popular sedative of all, alcohol) seldom provide a satisfactory solution to the problem of sleeplessness and it is all too common for the bereaved to become dependent on the drug without getting a satisfactory night's sleep. While it is true that an occasional sedative, such as nitrazepam, does little harm, regular reliance on sedatives for sleep tends to lead to bodily tolerance of the drug so that an increasing dosage is necessary to get the same effect. Prescribing a drug also gives doctors the illusion that they have solved the problem while, in fact, all they have done is to postpone it, and they may have created a new problem in the process.

Other avoidant strategies are to get rid of reminders of the lost person or even to sell up and move out of a district which is filled with so many painful reminders. We can sometimes help by advising people to avoid making irreversible changes in their lives which they may later regret. Some will consult social workers or doctors, demanding a certificate in support of rehousing on medical grounds. This is usually a short-sighted and ineffective policy, which may be bitterly regretted if the bereaved remove themselves from the social supports which will help them through their bereavement. It should be considered only if they are stuck in chronic grief and are moving to an area where the support is likely to be good.

Techniques for countering avoidance of grief

If our relationship with the person is good, and we have succeeded in creating a safe base, it is not unreasonable to go a little further. We can suggest to the client that there is some unfinished business to be done which involves the dead person. In order to bring the dead person symbolically into the room we may draw up an empty chair and say to the client, for example, 'Suppose your wife was sitting in that chair: what would you like to say to her?' We may then suggest what the dead person might have said in reply or, better, invite the client to change chairs and respond as if he or she were the person who died. This 'empty chair' technique is taken from Gestalt therapy and should not be used without previous practice in a training session. A similar technique is to ask bereaved people to write a letter to the deceased expressing their thoughts and feelings. These techniques are particularly useful if there is anger, guilt or other evidence of unresolved problems with the deceased, for instance if they have never said 'goodbye'. They are demonstrated in a training video by Franchino (1994).

Another technique is to invite the bereaved to bring photographs, or something belonging to the deceased, with them to the counselling session. While they are unlikely to do this if they are not ready to confront their loss, those who do often find it very cathartic to share their thoughts and feelings about such 'linking objects'.

One type of avoidance is to avoid emotions but not thoughts, and there are some people who are very 'out of touch' with their emotions. They will talk volubly about what has happened without showing anything. In such cases it often helps for the counsellor to ask, 'What did you feel about that?' or 'How does that make you feel?' This indicates clearly that *we* are not afraid to talk about feelings, a form of reassurance which may be quite lacking in this client's world. Another way of achieving the same ends is to suggest, 'I can't help feeling that, if I were in your shoes, I'd be very angry,' or, 'Listening to you, I feel sad' (or helpless or guilty and so on). This indicates to clients that if it is safe for us to have feelings it should be safe for them too.

Clients who use avoidant strategies are also likely to avoid bodily contact or other means of satisfying their needs for nurturance. We should be careful not to invade their personal space, but this does not mean that we should not make it perfectly clear that we are happy to touch or to get closer if they wish it. A touch of the hand or a smile at the right moment may be all that is needed to get across this important message. We should then watch carefully to see how clients respond. If they withdraw or frown we have clearly overstepped their boundaries, but no damage will have been done if we do not force ourselves upon them. On the other hand, a tentative gesture of support often leads to a more open acceptance of our willingness to help and the relationship may become more secure.

There is a small group whose avoidance of grieving may be so successful that everyone assumes that they have 'recovered'. Only years later, when some minor loss or trauma takes place, do they suddenly find themselves grieving intensely for a loss that occurred years previously.

Janet and Jim married young, just before the Second World War. Jim was called up and by the age of 22 had achieved the rank of captain. The war changed Jim, and Janet spent the rest of her life striving to find the man she had fallen in love with inside the distant, unfeeling person who had returned to her in 1945. After her death from cancer (age 60), the Macmillan nurse, Hazel, continued to visit Jim because she had been concerned by his ambivalent and at times angry relationship with Janet. Two months after his bereavement, while talking about the early days of his marriage, Jim suddenly 'became' the military officer he once was. He began to march around the house while talking about the men under his command. He had sent a group to clear a village after a shelling, the majority of whom had been killed in an explosion. Jim thought he had sent them to their deaths and he relived the experience of collecting up their bodily remains and writing to their families. Above all he recounted being condemned by the remaining soldiers for his lack of feeling.

Hazel walked beside him as he marched, listening without interrupting until he could relax enough to sit down and let the tears come. She recognized that the death of his wife had prompted these feelings to emerge and respected his sorrow without feeling the need to distract him. After this cathartic release Jim was able to talk about Janet and his recognition that their marriage had not met either of their needs. Several months later Jim planted two trees in his garden saying that he hoped that their roots would intertwine.

Post-Traumatic Stress and its Management

The term post-traumatic stress disorder (or PTSD) has received a lot of attention in recent years because, unlike pathological grief (which is contained within other categories), it has been deemed to be a psychiatric illness in its own right and sufferers can appropriately be referred for treatment to a psychiatric service.

The essential feature of PTSD is the existence of haunting memories or images of the traumatic event which intrude on the mind of the sufferer and evoke severe anxiety or panic. This is so unpleasant that it causes the sufferer to attempt to avoid all situations that might bring the traumatic event to mind. There are many bereaved people who have minor degrees of PTSD without meeting all of the criteria for a psychiatric diagnosis. Many of these will benefit from counselling and will not need referral to a specialist.

Intrusive memories are so common after bereavement as to be almost the rule rather than the exception. The only difference is that, whereas in PTSD these memories are dreaded and avoided, in typical grief they are cherished and treasured. Sudden, unexpected and untimely deaths, particularly if the survivor was present at the time and especially if also in serious danger, are particularly liable to give rise to PTSD.

The key to treatment seems to be to help sufferers to get back a feeling of being in control. They will do this, not by fighting against the thoughts and feelings – that just makes them worse – but by choosing to think about them and thereby regaining control of them. A clear example is the treatment of recurrent nightmares of the death, which recur partly *because* people go to bed dreading them. The bereaved need to be told that, while they cannot prevent the dream from occurring, they can influence how it will end. Having thought up a less horrifying end to the dream they will usually find that this puts them back in control and enables them to stop dreading the dream. When they stop dreading it the dream itself will stop recurring.

The treatment of intrusive memories is similar to that of recurrent dreams. The sufferer needs to discover that attempts to force such memories out of consciousness are doomed to disappointment, but by deliberately thinking about the memories one can bring them under control. One way of doing this is to go over the memory of the event again and again until the feeling associated with it begins to change. This relies on the fact that if we repeat anything often enough it becomes boring. Once the feeling has changed the bereaved can put the memory aside without it returning. This will not solve the problem permanently; the memory will certainly return again, but at least the bereaved person now has something to do about it and this increases confidence and leaves him or her more in control.

Chronic Grief and its Management

By chronic grief we mean a form of grieving which is severe from the start and which then persists for an abnormal length of time, sometimes for many years after the bereavement. Chronic grief causes more suffering than any other reaction to bereavement and it is usually associated with long-standing anxiety and depression. This may occur because the bereaved had a very intense, insecure attachment to the person who has died. These are commonly seen as 'dependent' but it is striking how often chronic grief can follow the death of the supposedly 'weaker' partner. It seems that, in many relationships, it is the function of the 'weaker' partner to reassure the 'strong' one of his or her own strength.

Jane (now aged 56) and her mother had both worshipped her father, seeing him as the strong member of the family. The middle one of three daughters (see Fig. 7.1), Jane had little confidence in women who, in her family, were all anxious and lacking in self-confidence. When Jane was 23 she married Henry (aged 32), a 'father figure' on whom she was very reliant. They had two daughters. Over the years Jane retained her strong attachment to

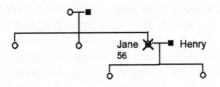

Figure 7.1 Genogram of Jane's family.

her father and was very upset when he moved to live in a distant town. For many years she telephoned him daily.

Seven years ago her father developed cancer and died a year later. Jane stayed with him during the last few months of his life and nursed him.

At the funeral she quarrelled with her sisters, whom she accused of neglecting their father. She grieved severely, but 'my husband helped me through'. Three years later he too was found to have cancer and Jane nursed him devotedly for another two years until his death. She then plummeted into severe grief, which showed little sign of abating when she was referred for bereavement counselling a year later.

At this time she could see no way in which she could survive without the two men whom she saw as having cared for and protected her. The fact that her daughters were devoted to her and that she had already demonstrated that she was not only well able to survive but capable of looking after the two men throughout their illnesses did not seem to have occurred to her. The most important thing that she needed from the counsellor (a man) was reassurance of her own strength. He consistently refused to advise her on any matter, referring all of her questions back to her: 'What do you think?' At the end of each session he would challenge her to suggest two or three things that she might do before the next meeting which would indicate to her that she was in control of her life and making progress. At first these were quite small things that most people would not have found difficult: inviting her sister to tea, or shopping in a department store on her own. Nothing succeeds like success. Before long Jane had joined a hiking club, where she made many friends. She discovered for the first time that it is not essential for a woman to have a man around in order to survive. Her confidence improved and her grief diminished.

*At the fourth session she responded positively when the coun-
sellor suggested that she would not need much more of his help.
She expressed some anxiety at the thought of ending the sessions
and there were some tears at their final meeting a month later.
But he had no doubt that she would cope without him and she
confirmed this five years later when they met by chance. Jane had
now become a social worker, she had been pioneering innovative
work and had written an article for publication about her work.
She recalled the counselling as a turning point in her life but an
alternative way of viewing this would be that the counselling had
simply helped her to recognize her own potential and that this
was something that it had been hard for her to do as long as she
had remained overshadowed by her father and her husband.*

Assessing and Managing Suicidal Risk

While it is rare for bereaved people to commit suicide, there is
sometimes an increased risk and it is important for us to be aware
of this and to do our best to prevent suicide. More commonly,
bereaved people will harm themselves by overdoses of drugs,
scratching their wrists, dangerous driving or other acts reflecting
their desperation or despair. This is sometimes termed 'para-
suicide'. It is not always obvious whether a particular act was an
attempt at suicide that failed or a para-suicide, and it is wise to
take seriously all such acts. Even if para-suicidal behaviour is
obviously a 'cry for help' rather than a serious suicidal attempt, it
reflects the fact that the person has got to the end of his or her
tether and is in need of help. This may sound obvious but people
admitted to hospital after a small overdose are often accused of
wasting the time of the medical staff and 'seeking attention' as if
this was an act of deliberate irresponsibility rather than one of
desperation.

Successful suicide[1] is most common among elderly bereaved
people who are socially isolated and suffering from clinical
depression (as described below) or other mental illness. If, in
addition, they are men rather than women, physically ill or

---

1 Para-suicide is more common among women rather than men, and younger
   people rather than older; it is associated with minor rather than major losses.

disabled, or if they are addicted to alcohol or other drugs the risk is increased. This said, there are some people who commit or attempt suicide after bereavement who are none of these things and others who have all of these risk factors but are not suicidal. Clearly, we need a more reliable indicator of risk and fortunately there is one. *The simple method of assessing suicidal risk is to ask the question, 'Has it been so bad that you have wanted to kill yourself?'* This question will almost always evoke an honest answer and counsellors should not hesitate to ask it whenever they have the least suspicion that someone may be at risk. Some counsellors are reluctant to raise the topic for fear they will put the idea into the client's head but we can be sure that, if people are *that* unhappy, they have thought of suicide. Whether or not there is a risk, we shall end up knowing.

There are some people who will reply to this question, 'I wouldn't care if I died tomorrow.' This is not necessarily an indication of an active intention to commit suicide. Those who are a serious risk will have worked out how they are going to kill themselves and are usually eager to talk about it. Once they do this it is usually obvious how immediate the risk is and what we need to do about it.

Hannah (50) was the only daughter of strictly religious Hungarian parents who came to England to take a university course. While here she met an English intellectual whom she subsequently married. She described it as a 'fairy tale' marriage but they had no children and five years later her husband died of a carcinoma of the lung, leaving her alone and friendless.

When seen in her large, empty, London flat she appeared depressed and restless, wringing her hands and crying profusely. She explained that she could not contemplate life without her husband and, when the counsellor asked if she had wanted to kill herself, she explained that she had a bottle of tablets in the cupboard and had several times looked at them and been tempted. Asked 'Do you think you might take them?' she answered 'Yes, yes – it's the only way.' Then she again burst into tears.

In cases such as this counsellors need to take immediate action to reduce the risk and to prevent it from arising again. In the short term this means removing the means to suicide if at all possible. If the client has a store of tablets it is best to remove them or to place them in the hands of a relative. But we should remember that in doing this we are removing our client's 'emergency exit' and it is important to leave something in its place. Instructions what to do 'if you get to the end of your tether' are important. It is often appropriate to leave the telephone number of the Samaritans or the hospice support team.

Once a bereaved person has 'spilled the beans' and confessed to suicidal thoughts there is usually a temporary reduction in the suicide risk and it is rare for counsellors to feel that they cannot safely leave the house of the suicidal client. This gives them time to take the next steps. Counsellors are ill advised to take the full burden of responsibility on their own shoulders and should *always* seek the help of others, *even if the client tries to persuade them not to*. This is one situation in which saving a life must take priority over any breach of confidentiality. In most instances the first person to talk to is a supervisor. The next person may be the client's GP, if there is one. If not, or if the GP agrees, referral to a psychiatrist is often the best course. Psychiatrists are used to assessing and handling suicidal risk and are in a position to treat any psychiatric disorder that may have been triggered by the bereavement. Counsellors should not, however, assume that their role is at an end after a referral has been made. They may need to check that the referral did actually lead to a consultation (a third of patients referred to a psychiatrist fail to keep their appointment) and the psychiatrist may be glad of the counsellor's continued support to the client, particularly if the psychiatrist decides to undertake treatment outside a hospital. There is often a time lag before antidepressant drugs become effective and close supervision and support may be needed during that time.

The client's family are the most valuable source of support in most cases and it is important to warn them of the risk and to solicit their help. They will often ensure that the client is not left alone and may remove the need for the client to be admitted to a psychiatric ward. In the event that admission is needed this should not be seen as a disaster. The great majority of bereaved people who threaten suicide will respond well to treatment and the minority who need in-patient care are unlikely to need to stay in hospital for more than a few weeks.

Hannah had no family in the United Kingdom and initially denied that she had any friends. She allowed the counsellor to remove all of the drugs in her medicine cupboard and agreed to accept referral to a psychiatrist. With the help of her GP, an appointment at the hospital was made the following day and the counsellor accompanied her to the hospital and talked to the psychiatrist. The psychiatrist admitted that there was a risk although he did not think that this was now immediate. He strongly advised Hannah to talk to her parents in Hungary about what was happening, but Hannah refused on the grounds that they were too far away to be of help and could not, at that time, leave the country. He asked the counsellor to continue to visit and to keep him informed of any developments.

When the counsellor visited Hannah on the following day she was surprised to find a neighbour in the house. This widowed lady lived in the same block and turned out to be a good friend. Hannah, in the depths of depression, had failed to mention this relationship or to realize its value but in the succeeding weeks it was this lady to whom she turned.

Before long it was clear that she was no longer seriously contemplating suicide and, although she always denied that she was any better (perhaps because she feared that she would then lose the help she needed), she returned to work on an academic thesis and eventually returned to Hungary to present a paper at a conference. This was a great success and, within a year, she had become quite well known in her homeland and was seriously thinking of returning to live there. She continued to live a lonely life but her academic success improved her morale and her depression gradually abated. She remained under occasional psychiatric supervision for a year and the counsellor continued to call with decreasing frequency for another three months thereafter.

From the counsellor's point of view, cases of this kind are very worrying. The counsellor needed to know that she could share the responsibility of care with the GP and psychiatrist. She also needed close support from her supervisor who, in this case, met regularly with her to review developments and was available to be consulted at other times if the need arose. The counsellor enjoyed her meetings with the psychiatrist who invited her, with Hannah's permission, to sit in on their interviews. This gave her an opportunity to share her own perceptions of what was going on and to reinforce the psychiatrist's attempts to reassure Hannah of her own worth and dignity (for Hannah was a very dignified person). They all ended up on good terms.

Depression and its Management

The word 'depression' has many meanings. To some it is synonymous with 'unhappiness'; to others it implies a specific psychiatric disorder. For the sake of clarity we shall use the term for any deep sorrow associated with feelings of helplessness and hopelessness.

One form of depression is 'clinical depression', which term we shall reserve for the psychiatric disorder characterized by slowing down of thoughts and movements, early morning waking, with deep depression which is at its worst at a particular time of day (usually the early morning), loss of appetite and weight, and profound feelings of self-reproach that are sometimes so intense as to reach delusional intensity (as when sufferers believe themselves to be the wickedest person in the world). It is important for counsellors to recognize this type of depression when they meet it because it will probably not respond to counselling and may be associated with a risk of suicide.

Clinical depression is one of the most miserable conditions that flesh is heir to and it is most important to ensure that it is treated as soon as possible. Fortunately, it usually responds well to antidepressant drugs and sufferers should be encouraged to comply with their doctor's orders if they are suffering from this condition. Most antidepressants take two to three weeks to become effective. During that time patients may experience side-effects and may be tempted to stop the drug on the grounds that it is doing more harm than good. They should be dissuaded if at all possible. Occasionally they may need to be admitted to a psychiatric unit for their own safety.

Antidepressant drugs are being used with increasing frequency as a treatment for depression, anxiety and panic disorders in bereaved people. Unlike the tranquillizers, they do not inhibit the expression of grief; in fact some people cannot begin to grieve until their depression has been treated. Nor are they habit forming; the fact that they take two to three weeks to work removes any temptation which people may have to 'pop' a tablet whenever they feel bad. They all have some side-effects, although people vary enormously in their sensitivity to these. Some have more side-effects than others, and people who cannot tolerate one antidepressant may well get on with a different one. Some of the older ones can be poisonous in overdose and close supervision may be needed if the bereaved person is potentially suicidal.

Lesser degrees of depression often respond well to counselling. The basic problem is one of motivation, and depressed people may need a lot of encouragement if they are to break out of the rut of depression. Depression causes people to give up and to get stuck in a rut of withdrawal and apathy. People often need to talk at length about the things that are depressing them. Having done this their distress may begin to subside, and at this point they may respond to a challenge: 'All right, things are bad; what are you going to do about it?' carries an implication that, however bad things may be, there is always something that *can* be done. It also implies that we have faith in the bereaved person's capacity to run his or her own life, make decisions and find new meanings.

It is important to challenge in the right way. A challenge is not a threat – 'Stop wasting my time or I'll reject you' – nor is it a facile injunction to 'Look on the bright side'. To be effective the challenge needs to be something that the bereaved person can recognize as reasonable, a target to be reached which will then stand as a sign of success and a starting point for the next challenge.

To depressed people life has little meaning and we cannot expect them to find that anything matters very much. But since life goes on they might as well do something that will eventually prove useful. The new meanings can only emerge from the wreckage of the old, but we may be surprised to find that not every good thing has gone from the world simply because one good person has died.

Many people are afraid to look forwards for fear that they will then forget the past. It may help them to realize that the future can be built upon the past. We are often brought closer to the people we have lost by doing the things that they would have done. The widow who learns to drive a car may feel closer to her lost husband when she is behind the wheel. The widower who never learned to cook may be surprised to feel close to his wife when he decides to do the cooking for himself. It helps to point out how our lives can be enriched by the memories of those we love. Bereaved people do not 'recover' from bereavement by forgetting the one they have loved, and we do not go back to being the person we were before we ever met them; if anything, we remember them better *because* we have recovered.

Louise (49) had never had much trust in herself or others. Teased and derided by her alcoholic father and distanced by a mother who could not stand being touched, she had grown up with little confidence that she could cope with life or that others would cope for her. Her first marriage had ended disastrously a few months later with the death of her husband due to heart disease. She remarried three months later and found in this relationship a mutually rewarding but interdependent relationship with a man who himself lacked confidence or trust in others. They had two children who eventually married and had families of their own.

Louise was always inclined to become depressed and had received medication for this condition in the past. Following the sudden and unexpected death of her second husband she plummeted into severe depression. She could not imagine how she could continue to live alone, yet her children had no room for her and none of them lived near at hand. She would wake early in the morning feeling suicidally depressed and afraid to face the day. She was apathetic and withdrawn. Talking to her was like wading through treacle and there was no way in which any effective psychotherapy could be carried out because her speech and thought were so slow. Her GP referred her to a psychiatrist who diagnosed clinical depression and prescribed amitriptyline, an antidepressant. He also arranged for her daughter to stay for a while and take charge of the medication.

Within three weeks the feelings of depression had abated and Louise was ready to talk. The psychiatrist encouraged her to contact her local bereavement service and she subsequently met with a counsellor who helped her to express her grief and encouraged her to venture out into the world. Her daughter stayed for three weeks and maintained daily contact with her by telephone, as did her other child. When last seen she said, 'I still miss my husband a lot but it's not as bad as it was'.

Anxiety and its Management

Anxiety is a normal feature of grief and all those who suffer a major loss should expect to feel tense and anxious and to suffer the physical symptoms which accompany anxiety and tension (as described on page 14). These are worst during the pangs of grief but continue in lesser degree at other times. Anxiety can become a problem if it is very severe or if it sets up a vicious circle of escalating fear and panic. Severe anxiety may arise in people who have always been nervous or in circumstances which are unusually frightening, such as when someone has witnessed an horrific or untimely death. Severe anxiety can be so unpleasant and unaccustomed that people who have had a panic attack in the street or on a train shut themselves up at home and refuse to go out. If they do go out they may have further attacks because they frighten themselves into the very condition that they dread. Having experienced one disaster in their lives people are often apprehensive that there is another round the corner. In this frame of mind they easily misinterpret the physical symptoms of anxiety as symptoms of illness.

Pauline (21) had never known her father and had been brought up by an alcoholic mother (Fig. 7.2); consequently she was not a secure girl. During her teens she was sent to a children's home for a while but subsequently her mother had stopped drinking and in recent years their relationship had improved. Two years ago she met and soon was cohabiting with and engaged to be married to Dennis.

During her mother's terminal cancer of the bladder Pauline was extremely anxious. She cried a great deal and found herself unable to concentrate on her work (trainee manager for British Rail). When her mother died she felt responsible for her mentally handicapped sister, and this added to her anxiety. She noticed that her heart was palpitating when she was lying in bed at night and this frightened her and caused her to fear that she too would die. She had difficulty in getting to sleep at night and began to get panic attacks during the day. At work she lost her temper with her boss and was told to take some time off.

She was seen by a counsellor and poured out the story of her life with copious tears. She brought photographs of her mother to the sessions and was able to express the very mixed feelings which had complicated their relationship. The counsellor explained to her the nature of her anxiety symptoms and reassured her that the palpitations were a sign that her heart was reacting normally to stress. She was given a tape recording of relaxation exercises to take home. These helped her to regain a sense of control over her

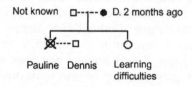

Figure 7.2 Pauline's genogram.

own anxiety and reduced her feelings of helplessness. At the same time the counsellor attempted to buttress her self-esteem by showing respect for her undoubted abilities and congratulating her on the care of her mother and sister.

Given this support she soon began to relax. When she did this her symptoms improved and this further increased her confidence. After only three sessions she was back at work, coping well and optimistic about the future. She continued to miss her mother but this was now a very normal reaction to bereavement and she required little further help.

Pauline's case illustrates well the ways in which anxiety can be managed. Positive reassurance of the normality of the anxiety along with an explanation for the symptoms which it produces in language which the client can understand are crucial. Instructions in relaxation help to put clients back in control and give them something they can do when they feel most helpless. Respect and reassurance of personal worth does more good than pity (which only serves to make bereaved people feel more inferior than they already do). At the same time we must respect their need to grieve, and give them every opportunity to share this.

Anger and Guilt

Feelings of irritability and self-reproach are common reactions to bereavement and often go together. Like anxiety and minor degrees of depression, they are a normal part of grief. They can become a problem if they are unusually severe, in which case they may cause people to alienate others who might support them and to engage in self-punitive grieving: 'Why should I be happy now that he is dead?'

Some bereavements are a reasonable cause for anger and we should not assume that all anger is irrational. Having said that, there is often an unreasonable component to the most reasonable anger. People easily get things out of proportion, blame the wrong people and may even engage in vindictive threats or attacks on people whose behaviour does not justify it. Doctors and nurses are particularly liable to such attacks, which often take the form of complaints against the people who provided care for the person who is now dead.

Sarah was 28 years of age when her baby daughter died suddenly and unexpectedly from congenital heart disease. The disease had been diagnosed at birth but the baby had not been incapacitated and Sarah had no idea that her life was at risk. After her death she blamed the doctors for failing to recognize the seriousness of the condition and, at the time when she was referred for counselling, she was threatening to kill a paediatrician. She was also complaining of recurrent nightmares of her baby dying.

Sarah had learned to look after herself from an early age and, as a friend put it, she 'Goes through life with her fists up'. Physically abused by her black Caribbean father as a child and distrustful of her white depressive mother, she had been a very rebellious teenager and had got into trouble for promiscuity and prostitution. She tended to drink too much and her relationship with her daughter's father was stormy.

She was initially extremely suspicious of the counsellor to whom she was referred, but soon relaxed when he proved willing to listen to her complaints without arguing with her. In no time she was pouring out the story of her life and the counsellor was able to agree that she had a great deal to feel angry about. He suggested that there is nothing good or bad about anger but it can have good or bad consequences, depending on how it is expressed. Sarah was surprised to hear this, as she had been taught that all anger and rebellion are wicked and she thought of herself as a wicked girl. In fact she expressed a surprising amount of guilt for the bad things that she had done in the past. The counsellor, on the other hand, came to appreciate her courage and her gutsy refusal to be defeated by life.

A meeting was arranged with the paediatrician who had cared for her baby and she conducted herself well during this, having been advised by her counsellor to prepare the questions she wanted to ask beforehand. Rather to her surprise the paediatrician apologized to her for failing to realize the risk to her daughter and this disarmed her anger. Subsequently she was able to put her anger aside and it soon became clear that Sarah was longing for the love which she had never had as a child. Her partner, who had found her irritability hard to tolerate, was asked by the counsellor why he had stuck by her. He replied that he loved her very much even though, at times, he also came close to hating her. Sarah, who understood from her own experience the nature of ambivalence, found this reassuring.

A few weeks later she again became pregnant and this did more than anything else to enable her to let go of her grief for the child who had died.

When last seen, she had stopped drinking, her nightmares were now rare and she was overjoyed at the prospect of a new baby. It would, perhaps, be unrealistic to imagine that all of her problems were at an end or that she would live happily ever after, but the counsellor felt that she was now on course towards a more satisfactory adjustment to life.

In such cases it is important for the counsellor to avoid judging the client. We do not have to agree with clients' attempts to blame others but we must avoid taking sides against them. It is often possible to convey our understanding for the anger without approving the irrational behaviour to which it may have given rise. Anger is always justified; its consequences may not be. As we have seen, when people explain themselves to us they are also explaining themselves to themselves. To understand is to forgive, and this can apply to ourselves as well as to others.

Guilt is another emotion which can have good or bad consequences, depending on how it is expressed. It is most likely to cause problems if a person becomes persuaded that he or she was responsible for the death of a loved person. One of the reasons that confession is good for the soul is that the person who confesses may thereby get a different perspective on the sin. As with anger, it is important for the client to tell the story in full detail and it is important for the counsellor not to argue. This can be quite hard when we think that guilt is irrational, and it is very difficult not to say, 'You shouldn't feel guilty about that.' A more fruitful response takes the form of a challenge: 'If that is how you feel, what can you do about it?' This again faces the bereaved person with the possibility that guilt can be a creative as well as a destructive emotion and challenges him or her to think of a more creative way of expressing it.

Flora (38) was driving her widowed mother in her car and turning right into a major road when the car came into collision with another vehicle. This ran into the passenger side of her car, killing her mother instantly.

Flora was uninjured but she blamed herself and, although no charges were brought against her, the police made it clear that they did not blame the other driver. Six months later she was still preoccupied with feelings of guilt, afraid to go out for fear that people would criticize her and unable to speak to her sister because she thought that her sister must blame her for killing their mother.

She stayed in bed most of the day and was fearful of going back to her work as a teacher because she did not think she could be responsible for caring for young people and feared that they too would die if she did. Her first attempt to obtain counselling came to an abrupt end when her counsellor suggested that she was 'Not yet ready to get better'. This dismissive remark provoked her to break off counselling and to return to work, but further aggravated her feelings of guilt, which were still very pronounced when she sought the help of another counsellor six months later.

Her second counsellor expressed neither praise nor blame. When asked directly what he thought about the accident, he said, 'I suppose what happened to you is what everybody who drives a car dreads most, the thought that we might be driving in an accident in which someone is killed. I can't judge you because I was not there at the time and I cannot know whether or not I would have behaved in the same way if I had been driving. None of us is perfect. Perhaps the important question is not whether you killed her but whether you intended to kill her?' To this question Flora answered an emphatic 'No'. The conversation then turned to the question of what she could do about the guilty feelings that she continued to experience. She said, 'Well I suppose I don't deserve to be happy.' The counsellor quoted Hamlet: 'Use every man after his desert and who should 'scape whipping?', and then asked her what she might do about this guilty feeling.

This conversation proved very fruitful and, by the time of her next visit, Flora had decided on two courses of action: she would ask a priest to make a formal blessing at her mother's grave and invite her sister to come; she would also do voluntary work for a children's organization. When she told her sister of her plan for the blessing, her sister remonstrated with her, suggesting that she was only going to pour salt into her wounds and that it would be more sensible to forget what had happened. She made it clear that she did not blame Flora and did not see the necessity for this action. Flora, on the other hand, felt very strongly that this was an important thing to do and was relieved when her sister agreed to take part. The event proved very moving to them both and restored the loving relationship which existed between them. Many of their friends came to the blessing and Flora had a strong feeling that she was making public restitution for what she had done. Thereafter her distress diminished and she was able to return to a useful and rewarding life. She had no further need for counselling.

Alcohol and Drug Abuse

Should we regard the consumption of drugs or alcohol as a treatment for grief or a problem to be solved? Most bereaved people will make use of one or other of the many drugs available to us, be it an aspirin, a tranquillizer or a glass of whisky. Taken in moderation none of these things is harmful and may even make us feel better. A single whisky before bed may help someone to relax and sleep; an aspirin may relieve a headache or a tranquillizer enable us to cope with a dental appointment or an important job interview. Drugs do work and it is not surprising that many bereaved people go to their doctors at some time or other in order to seek relief from some of the pains of grief. The problem is that no drug can solve the basic problem of grieving. Grief seems to be a job of work which we need to do. Drugs can be used as a means to escape for a time from that work, but the work still has to be done.

It is tempting for people to imagine that, because they feel less pain when they take a drug, they can go on taking the drug and increase the dose to the point where the pain is avoided altogether. The fallacy is soon apparent. Not only does the drug cease to have the effect that was intended as we grow accustomed to it, but we soon become increasingly reliant on the drug. This is particularly the case with tranquillizers such as diazepam (Valium) or alcohol (the two drugs are not dissimilar in their effects). It is an all too common experience that people who start using these drugs to relieve anxiety soon find that they need to increase the dose in order to maintain the benefit. A time comes when any attempt to reduce the dose gives rise to the very symptoms that the drug was intended to relieve. Withdrawal of alcohol or diazepam then produces severe anxiety, which can be relieved only by reverting to the drug – the person is 'hooked'.

'Hard drugs' such as morphine, cocaine or codeine are even more addictive but they account for only a small proportion of the people who develop drug problems after bereavement. Alcohol, unlike morphine, is socially accepted in our society. In fact bereaved people may find themselves under some pressure to 'Have a drink, you'll feel better.' There are still some doctors who prescribe regular doses of diazepam and similar drugs for bereaved people despite the fact that the drug companies themselves warn against this.

Night sedatives are hard to resist if only because sleeping can be so difficult after bereavement. The fact that nobody has yet died of lack of sleep and most people do not actually need more than four hours' sleep at night does not prevent some people from worrying a great deal if they do not get their habitual eight hours. Having found a sedative which will knock them out, it is tempting to take this every night. Before long they are hooked and asking for a larger dose. The more people worry about not sleeping the worse they sleep.

The counsellor can help by encouraging people not to take their drug every night, by reassuring them that they do not need to worry about sleep and by helping them to control anxiety as indicated above. A relaxation tape can be a great sedative.

Those who, despite our best endeavours, find themselves dependent on drugs may need to be referred to one of the organizations that specialize in helping people with such problems.

It is a sad fact of life that many of those who need help with drug problems are the last to ask for it, and without the motivation to get help they are likely to be difficult to help. Drugs attract people who are seeking an easy way out of the problem of grief and the truth is there is no such thing. They may have to find out for themselves that they are caught in a trap before it is possible to help them out of it. That said, there are many people who do eventually recognize their need for help with a drug problem and there is then a great deal that can be done to help them.

Martin was not normally a regular drinker but he had a long history of 'bingeing' at times of trouble. When his teenage son died from inhaling butane gas, Martin immediately started drinking heavily. He had always had difficulty in expressing emotions but when he was drunk he would cry profusely and he said that alcohol helped him to grieve. Unfortunately he also became very aggressive when he drank and he asked for help only after his wife could stand it no longer and walked out on him.

Martin knew that she would eventually visit their son's grave, so he waited for her at the grave side until she arrived and she then agreed to come back to him if he would accept counselling. The counsellor suggested that the two of them attend together, and it was soon apparent that they were both in need of support.

Given the opportunity to talk through their grief and to share their feelings of anger and sadness with a third party they drew closer. Martin spoke of the physical abuse and neglect which he had experienced at the hands of both his parents. His wife related similar feelings of rejection. Their similar histories explained why they lacked confidence in themselves and others but it also helped them to understand each other and to become more tolerant of each other.

Once he began to feel more secure, Martin succeeded in reducing his consumption of alcohol and, while he did not give it up altogether, he made a rule only to drink with his wife and to accept her judgement when to stop. They both had a lot of grieving to do, but now each felt that they had no need to hide their grief from their partner and this seemed to make things easier.

Special Situations

The many different types of bereavement give rise to many different patterns of grief, some more problematic than others. Among the most traumatic are bereavements by suicide, homicide and disasters. Each of these is likely to cause one or more of the types of problem listed above, and some add others of their own. It would take us beyond the scope of this book to attempt a detailed account of the multiple effects of each type of situation. Instead, we shall simply point up some of the particular difficulties which arise and discuss the implications of these for the provision of counselling. The reader who wishes to know more should consult a specialist work on the subject, several of which are referenced here.

Bereavement by suicide

Bereavement by suicide is often unexpected, violent, and untimely. It follows that it is also often a cause of anxiety and post-traumatic stress. Because it is the voluntary choice of the person who dies, it usually gives rise to mixed feelings of anger and guilt in the survivors. Why did the person do this? Was it the survivor's fault? Was it intended to punish us? Why didn't we prevent it?

There are many kinds of suicide and not all of them are unexpected and untimely. In some cases the person has been mentally ill for a great length of time and has suffered a great deal. His or her death may have been expected again and again. When it finally takes place the reaction may be one of relief. More often the death has not been expected. Even though most people who commit suicide have warned somebody of their intention, their warning has been disbelieved or ignored. It follows that people bereaved by suicide are often in need of counselling and every opportunity should be taken to ensure that those who need help will get it. This is easier said than done, for suicide carries a stigma and those whom it has touched do not necessarily feel themselves entitled to ask for help. Their friends are embarrassed by them and the social support normally available to the bereaved is often missing. The suicide becomes a skeleton in the family cupboard and is dealt with by avoiding the problem rather than talking about it.

As with other stigmatized groups, the relatives of people who have died by suicide may feel more comfortable talking to others who are 'in the same boat' than to doctors, counsellors and others who are not themselves stigmatized. This means that there is a need for group help for the survivors of suicide and this has proved a successful method of providing counselling.

Some people commit suicide when a secret about which they feel guilty has been found out. A sexual habit or relationship, a large debt or a criminal act may all cause people to kill themselves when the secret is revealed. They may leave behind major problems for their surviving relatives, not the least of which is the problem of understanding why they felt they had to conceal an important part of their lives from their nearest family and friends.

In such cases it is important for the bereaved to re-examine their perceptions of the person who died and their relationship with them. 'Who was this person? Why didn't they trust us with their secret? Why didn't we know what was going on?' Questions of this kind are bound to arise and, although it may not be possible to find satisfactory answers, the honest appraisal of the relationship may cause the survivors to learn from any mistakes that have been made.

For a fuller account of the problems of bereavement by suicide the reader is recommended to read Wertheimer (1991).

Murder and manslaughter

Murder and manslaughter are probably the most traumatic causes of bereavement. Unfortunately space does not permit an examination of the special problems to which they give rise and the interested reader is referred to Hendriks *et al.* (1993), Redmond (1989) and Parkes (1993).

As in the case of bereavement by suicide, people bereaved by murder can expect to be understood and helped by others in the same situation. Some organizations offering mutual help of this kind are listed in Appendix 1.

Disasters

Disasters can be arbitrarily defined as traumatic losses involving ten or more deaths or extensive destruction. They differ from other types of traumatic bereavement in the chaos which inevitably results and the overwhelming impact of the event on both victims and helpers. The magnitude of the trauma is so great that everybody is likely to see themselves as at the centre of the disaster (the so-called illusion of centrality) and demands for help usually quickly outstrip the help available. Although modern methods of communication soon bring news of a disaster to the rest of the world and would-be helpers pour into the area, this may simply add to the chaos. Telephone lines become blocked, rescue work is hampered and some people find themselves visited by too many 'counsellors' while others receive no help at all.

Because disasters are always unexpected we tend to be unprepared for them. Emergency services are well used to planning in advance for disasters and every hospital has its disaster plan. Yet these plans seldom include psychosocial care. We believe that this is a mistake and that much can be done to prepare for disasters and to ensure a rapid response if and when the need arises. In the United Kingdom an advanced plan for for disaster management has been prepared by a government working party and we recommend that this be studied by all of those responsible for bereavement and other psychosocial services (Allen, 1990). Essentials to be planned in advance and provided immediately in response to most disasters are an office/information centre near to the site of the disaster, a dedicated team of trained professionals, a telephone hot line, a database to record details of all victims, survivors, bereaved families and would-be helpers and an information/press officer.

While many organizations for the bereaved rely upon self-referral, the risk to psychological health is so great following a disaster that active outreach to all survivors and bereaved families is needed. This should ensure that everyone who may need help has met someone from a team who has been trained to assess their needs and to advise them about what is available.

The skills needed to help in a disaster area are not essentially different from those needed following road traffic accidents and other traumatic events. They include bereavement counselling, anxiety management and the identification and management of post-traumatic stress. Training in these should be a part of the basic training of all bereavement counsellors and members of the caregiving professions.

Help is likely to be needed by survivors, who may or may not be bereaved, and by bereaved relatives. More than anywhere else the helper is likely to feel overwhelmed by the sheer magnitude of the losses involved, and it is important to remember that neither we nor the bereaved are capable of dealing with more than one problem at a time. Time spent in considering priorities and deciding what must be dealt with now and what can be put aside until later is important.

Numbness and disbelief, which are common following all traumatic bereavements, are likely to be particularly pronounced after a disaster. They often enable traumatized people to help in rescue operations and some may even be found offering counselling to others, although it is soon apparent that their thought and behaviour are less well organized than they should be. More often people are dazed and bewildered by the situation; they may wander about in a fitful way or wait passively to be told what to do. Despite this passivity, anger is seldom far from the surface and easily breaks out. This may be particularly directed at people who are thought to be to blame for the disaster and can include anyone in authority. Rumours abound and the counsellor would be wise to treat with scepticism most of the 'explanations' for the disaster which are current in the early stages. We may need to persuade people not to take drastic actions which may add to the problems of those who are trying to restore control.

There is a great temptation for counsellors to take on too much. In consequence we run the risk that we shall get tired, make mistakes and may even become depressed and burn out. It is, therefore, important for counsellors to monitor themselves and each other. Appropriate rest periods and debriefing are essential.

Debriefing is the term used for group sessions in which helpers, be they members of rescue services, police or counsellors, meet together in the presence of a trained group leader in order to take stock and to provide mutual support to each other. It can also be used to support groups of people who have been involved in other ways with a disaster but are not themselves severely traumatized. This can include bystanders, people near the periphery of a disaster and others who do not need or wish for more intensive types of counselling. Debriefing is not counselling or therapy.

Typically, a debriefing session will start with an introductory phase in which the group leader will explain the purpose of the exercise and the members of the group will introduce themselves and explain how they came to be involved. Emphasis is placed on the importance of treating everything said in the group as confidential unless the group members have authorized disclosure of particular information (such as lessons to be learned from the disaster). Each member is then asked to describe what happened to him or her during the disaster. Some group leaders adopt a structured approach, moving from the discussion of facts, to thoughts and then feelings about what happened. We prefer a more spontaneous approach, allowing group members to decide upon the group's priorities and intervening only if the group becomes bogged down or dominated by one particular individual or faction. It is important that everybody has the opportunity to be heard, even though some may prefer to remain silent.

If participants report symptoms of PTSD, grief or other types of reaction, it is useful for the leader to explain something of the nature of these symptoms and, in particular, to reassure people, where appropriate, of the normality of their reactions. Towards the end of the session, which should normally last about an hour and a half, the leader may attempt to summarize the lessons that have been learned and indicate the way people should expect things to go in the short term. The group may need to make plans for their further involvement and will sometimes wish to issue a report to those in authority. This should be done only with the full agreement of the group.

Group leaders should make themselves available after the group and it is often desirable to see each of the members briefly to give them a chance to talk about anything that they did not wish to discuss in front of the group. If circumstances permit it is usually desirable to hold one or more follow-up groups at a later date. Any members who need counselling should be referred on an individual basis.

However well prepared the team may think they are, there is always a need for *further assessment and training* after the disaster has taken place. Among other things, a day conference to enable all those who are providing psychosocial care to take stock of the situation and check what else is needed should be organized as soon as practical arrangements can be made. It is of great value to invite professionals and researchers with experience of this field.

The sooner counselling can be provided, the sooner it will no longer be needed. Counselling can usually be phased out progressively during the second to third years after the disaster, after which time any residual needs for care can be met by existing social and mental health services. Those involved in providing counselling following disasters will be changed by the experience and may not wish to return to the roles which they formerly performed. Their experience will have made them a valuable resource to other victims of trauma and bereavement and they should be given all the encouragement and help they need to put these skills to use.

Disasters vary greatly and no one plan can meet all possible situations. For an analysis of the main types of disaster and their implications for planning see Parkes (1991), and for a more extended treatment of the whole topic see the specialist textbooks by Raphael (1986) and Hodgkinson and Stewart (1991).

As in other situations of loss, the provision of prompt and effective counselling should reduce the risk of psychiatric problems. In this field, as in many others, prevention is better than cure, and the costs of neglecting the care of traumatized individuals can be enormous.

Summary

❑ Much avoidance of grief is normal and becomes a problem only if excessive. It may then cause nightmares, panic attacks, depression and physical symptoms.

❑ Techniques which can be used to help clients to grieve include the use of an empty chair for the dead person, discussing photographs and mementoes of the dead person, inviting clients to tell us how they feel, and sensitive use of non-verbal means of communication.

❑ Post-traumatic stress disorder is a recognized psychiatric disorder which often follows traumatic bereavements. In its full form it requires psychiatric treatment and may entitle people to compensation.

❑ Chronic grief is the commonest complication of grief. It most often arises in people with little confidence in their ability to survive without the one who has died. Counselling will succeed only if it enables the bereaved to discover their true potential.

❑ Counsellors should not hesitate to ask directly if a bereaved person is tempted to commit suicide.

❑ Whenever a client is thought to be at risk of suicide counsellors should seek advice, even if the client has asked them not to. Psychiatric referral should always be considered.

❑ Clinical depression usually responds well to medical treatment and is unlikely to respond to counselling alone.

❑ Anxiety is a normal feature of grief that easily becomes self-perpetuating. It usually responds well to explanation, reassurance, relaxation training and respect for personal worth.

❑ Anger and guilt can cause problems if severe and may cause people to get things out of proportion.

❑ Alcohol and other tranquillizers and sedatives are popular but habit forming and may lead to tolerance.

❑ People bereaved by suicide, murder or manslaughter are often in need of counselling.

❑ The risk to psychological health is so great following a disaster that an active outreach to all survivors and bereaved families is needed.

❑ Training in bereavement counselling, anxiety management and the identification and management of post-traumatic stress should be part of the basic training of all bereavement counsellors and members of the caregiving professions.

❑ Critical incident stress debriefing should be provided to all rescue and emergency staff as well as provision of regular supervision and support to counsellors.

❑ In the field of disasters, as in many others, prevention is better than cure and the costs of neglecting the care of traumatized individuals can be enormous.

8

Conclusions

In this book we have focused on the counselling which is needed by patients and families at times of death and bereavement, but many of the principles that we have adopted and the techniques which are useful in these settings also have value in other circumstances. Grief, fear and other powerful emotions are experienced by many patients and family members when nobody is dying, and death is only one of the painful turning points in family life which come to the attention of the providers of health care. The amputation of a limb, the loss of sight or hearing, the onset of dementia can all have profound effects on patients and their families. If we accept the role, propounded in Chapter 2, that professional carers are agents of change, then we need to take every opportunity to help at such times. It would, however, take us beyond the remit of this book to attempt a thorough account of the psychological aspects of rehabilitation. Instead, we will simply restate some of the basic lessons which have emerged in the course of this book and examine how they can be applied in these other settings (a more detailed exposition of the field is given by Markus *et al.*, 1989).

The Family is the Unit of Care

The wife who has to retire from work in order to look after a disabled or dementing husband, the mother who is told that her child has a permanent disability, with a mental age of four, and the husband who discovers that his wife has lost interest in sex, all suffer griefs that may be just as severe as those associated with terminal illness and bereavement by death. Similarly, the lasting uncertainty and threat which hang over the family of a middle-aged man who has had his second episode of coronary ischaemia or the parents of a child with chronic renal disease match those which confront a family invaded by cancer or AIDS.

It follows that we should place the needs of the family, which includes the patient, at the forefront of our concern. They are the ones on whom the success or failure of rehabilitation will often rest. They need to be included in our plans, supported through their griefs, reassured where possible and taken into partnership with us. They are both the carers and the cared for. It is as illogical to exclude the patient's wife from the physiotherapy department as it is to exclude her from the bedside of a dying husband. Time and again we shall find that the family are our best allies or our worst enemies in our attempts to help our patients to start a new life. An over-anxious wife can undermine her husband's attempts to walk without a stick; a depressed husband can drag down his disabled wife and discourage her from doing the things she needs to do if she is to resume control of her life. Parents who over-protect a child with a disability may prevent that child from becoming autonomous. Any of these consequences may be prevented if proper regard is paid to the needs of the family. The genogram remains the first and most important tool in this endeavour and opens the door to our care for the family.

Fear and Grief are Normal Reactions

As in the reactions of patients and their families to terminal illness, the fear and grief which accompany other frightening or disabling diseases or injuries are to be expected and may aggravate themselves. People need explanation, reassurance, permission to express their feelings, and emotional support if they are to live with these distressing reactions.

Just as it is normal for a widow to hallucinate about the presence of a dead husband, so it is normal for the amputee to hallucinate about the presence of a 'phantom limb'. Palpitations are a normal physiological accompaniment of fear but they are easily misinterpreted if a person has heart disease. Anxiety is normally associated with an increase in muscle tension and, if this goes on for any length of time, the affected muscles begin to ache. If the sufferer then worries about the ache, focusing attention on an affected part and trying to 'fight' the pain, the pain will get worse. Conversely, warning amputees before their operation that they will continue to feel as if their limb is present afterwards, reassuring cardiac patients that the palpitations that accompany anxiety are a sign that the heart is functioning normally, instructing those who mistake a tension pain for an organic one in relaxation of tense muscles and explaining the physiological causes of the pain are all likely to prevent or break vicious circles that may be set up.

Help for Vulnerable People and Families

As we have seen, vulnerable or excessively traumatized people may avoid facing up to a loss or they may become obsessively preoccupied with it. Just as excessive avoidance of grief can complicate the course of recovery after bereavement, producing inhibited or chronic reactions, so it can following other losses. The rehabilitation of blind people is frequently delayed by their difficulty in accepting the fact that they are blind, and deaf people often blame their hearing aid rather than accepting that their hearing is getting worse. The caregiver must recognize these symptoms for what they are – attempts to postpone the pain of grief. Rather than blaming patients and putting pressure on them, thereby increasing their fear, we will get better results if we take time and trouble to get to know them and understand the nature of their fears. While we are doing this we will be creating the kind of secure base from which they will subsequently feel safe enough to confront their fears.

Excessive preoccupation with painful memories and fears may also occur. Thus anxious and insecure people who have been subjected to open heart surgery often become 'cardiac cripples', remaining anxiously apprehensive and fearful of the least exertion, despite the fact that their cardiac function is now normal. Their image of themselves as permanently damaged and in danger of a painful death may prevent them from collaborating with exercise programmes aimed at restoring the strength of their heart and other muscles and helping them to return to a normal life. Again, counselling is more likely to be effective if the counsellor recognizes that the very symptoms that are seen by the doctors as endangering the patient's recovery are seen by the patient as ways of staying alive. To remain immobile and on one's guard feels like the right way to behave when any shock or exertion may kill you. The fact that the doctor tells you that you are out of danger may not convince a person who has established a very different way of viewing the world. Counsellors stand very little chance of changing patients' minds unless they respect them enough to understand their point of view. Again, the establishment of a relationship of trust is the first requirement; only then can patients be expected to place their lives in our hands.

Vulnerable families, as we have seen, may find any change, even a change for the better, a threat to an established homeostasis. A wife who has found a rewarding and dominant role as caregiver to a disabled husband may find it hard to give up that role when he is no longer disabled and may find ways to undermine his rehabilitation. Similarly, a man who has never had much confidence in his ability to cope may play up his disabilities in order to maintain his position as the 'baby' of the family. Other family members may collude with this for their own reasons and create a situation which is impervious to rehabilitation. In such cases it is unlikely that counselling any one individual will change anything, but group meetings with the family, as described on pages 153–154, do hold out hope of helping each member to feel safe enough to weigh up the advantages and disadvantages of changing the situation.

The Team's Own Needs for Support

However rewarding the counselling which we have been advocating may be, it will only become a burden to sensitive and caring staff if they do not have the time, the sanction or the support to do it properly. Time, training and sanction for counselling need to be built into any system of health care worthy of the name, as do proper systems of support for staff. This is not a luxury or a waste of valuable staff time.

The Need for Counselling

Every health care system is burdened with large numbers of chronically sick patients for whom care is very costly. The right counselling given at the right time by the right person can prevent much of this chronicity. Nor does the counselling have to be costly. Much of it does not require the use of expensive psychiatrists or psychologists – it can be given by properly trained nurses and, very often, by volunteers.

Sooner or later all members of a society will meet situations of danger and loss in their lives. While many will cope with these dangers and losses on their own, and others with the help of their families, there will always be a substantial minority of us who will need help from outside the family. If this help is not forthcoming our health and future ability to cope is at risk and the future of our family may also be in jeopardy. If, on the other hand, a little help is given in the right way we shall emerge stronger and wiser than we were when first we met the danger or experienced the loss. These are the turning points of life and the test of a caring community. They are also a good investment.

Summary

❑   Fear and grief are ubiquitous and arise in many situations other than those which are associated with terminal illness and bereavement.

❑   It follows that members of the health care professions and volunteers have many opportunities to help people through the turning points in their lives which result from illness and disability.

Appendix 1: List of Organizations for Terminally Ill and Bereaved People

United Kingdom

BACUP, 3 Bath Place (off Rivington Street), London EC2A 3JR
Tel: 0171 613 2121
Information given by trained cancer nurses, together with practical advice and emotional support. Publications on different types of cancer.

Cancerlink, 17 Brittania Street, London WC1X 9JN
Tel: 0171 833 2451
Information given by trained staff on all aspects of cancer. Resource service for cancer support and self-help groups.

Compassionate Friends, 53 North Street, Bedminster, Bristol BS3 1EN
Tel: 0117 953 9639; Fax: 0117 966 5202
A nationwide self-help organization of parents whose child of any age, including adult, has died from any cause. Personal and group support. A quarterly newsletter, a postal library and a range of leaflets are published. A befriending and not a counselling service.

Cruse: Bereavement Care, Cruse House, 126 Sheen Road, Richmond, Surrey TW9 1UR
Tel: 0181 940 4818
Bereavement Line 09:30–17:00; Tel: 0181 332 7227
A national organization for anyone who has been bereaved. Offers a counselling service to help with the emotional difficulties of bereavement and offers practical advice. A network of local branches exists throughout the UK.

Hospice Information Service, St Christopher's Hospice, 51 Lawrie Park Road, Sydenham, London SE26 6DZ
Provides comprehensive information about hospice services which indicates those that provide bereavement services.

Lesbian and Gay Bereavement Project, Vaughan M. Williams Centre, Colindale Hospital, London NW9 5GH
Helpline: Tel: 0181 455 8894; Fax: 0181 905 9250
Telephone counselling for lesbians and gay men bereaved by the loss of a same-sex partner, or otherwise affected by bereavement; a

member is on duty from 19:00 to midnight. Publishes will form, and often find suitable clergy or secular officiants for funerals.

National Association of Bereavement Services, 20 Norton Folgate, London E1 6DB
Tel\Fax: 0171 247 0617
Referrals: Tel: 0171 247 1080
Provides information about bereavement services, publishes a directory of bereavement services in the UK and a newsletter (*Lifeline*) and organizes conferences and training events.

OXAIDS, 43 Pembroke Street, Oxford OX1 1BP
Tel: 01865 243 389, Helpline 0800 393 999 (free 6:30–20:30); Fax: 01865 792 210
HIV-related support and education in Oxfordshire including Buddying, groups, Gay Men's Project and special funds.

SAMM (Support After Murder and Manslaughter), Cranmer House, 39 Brixton Road, London SW9 6DZ
Tel: 0171 735 3838; Fax: 0171 735 3900

Samaritans
Tel. 0171 734 2800
Always there at any hour of the day or night to offer confidential emotional support to those in crisis and in danger of taking their own lives. There are 200 centres in the UK and Republic of Ireland.

SANDS (Stillbirth and Neonatal Death Society)
Tel: 0171 436 5881

Australasia

Australian Association for Hospice and Palliative Care Inc., PO Box 1200, North Fitzroy, Victoria 3068, Australia
Tel: 61 3 486 2666; Fax: 61 3 482 5094
A national association consulting with government and health authorities on behalf of all palliative care services. A Directory of Hospice and Palliative Care Services in Australia is published on behalf of this Association by:

South Australian Association for Hospice and Palliative Care, PO Box 275, Belair, SA 5052, Australia
Tel: 61 8 278 7402; Fax: 61 8 278 3944

Hospice New Zealand, PO Box 12481, Wellington, New Zealand
Tel: 61 4 473 3159; Fax: 61 4 278 3944
Promotes the principles of hospice and palliative care among
health professionals and the general public and acts as the
coordinating body for the Hospice movement in New Zealand.

National Association for Loss and Grief, PO Box 460, Lane Cove,
New South Wales, NSW 2066, Australia
Tel: 02 517 0241; Fax: 02 427 4668

North America

Association for Death Education and Counselling, 638 Prospect
Avenue, Hartford, Connecticut 06105-4298, USA
Tel: 203 586 7503; Fax: 203 586 7550
An international, interdisciplinary organization concerned with
death, dying and bereavement.

Canadian Palliative Care Association, Suite 112, 43 Bruyere Street,
Ottawa, Ontario, K1N 5C8, Canada
Tel: 613 560 1483; Fax: 613 560 1487
Promotes the philosophy and principles of palliative care in
Canada.

Candlelighters Childhood Cancer Foundation, 7910 Woodmont
Avenue, Ste 460, Bethesda, MD 20814, USA
Tel: 800 366 2223; 301 718 2686
An international network of groups of parents of children with
cancer.

Children's Hospice International, 2202 Mount Vernon Avenue,
Suite 3-C, Alexandria, VA 22301, USA
Tel: 703 684 0330
Provides medical, psychological, social, and spiritual support to
terminally ill children and their families.

Compassionate Friends, PO Box 3696, Oak Brook, IL 60522-3696,
USA
Tel: 708 990 0010
National organization that supports and aids parents in the
positive resolution of the grief experienced upon the death of their
child.

Hospice Education Institute, 190 Westbrook Road, Essex, Connecticut 06426, USA
Tel: 203 767 1620; Fax: 203 767 2746

In addition to its database of US hospices, provides free telephone advice and support service (HOSPICE LINK 800 331 1620) for the general public and offers continuing education for health professionals.

National Hospice organization, 1901 North Moore Street, Suite 901, Arlington, Virginia 22209, USA
Tel: 703 243 5900

In addition to publishing the *Guide to the Nation's Hospices*, provides hospice referral services to the general public (tel: 1-800 658 8898) as well as educational programmes, technical assistance, publications and advocacy.

Other international sources of help

European Association for Palliative Care, National Cancer Institute, Milan, Via Venezian 1, 20133 Milan, Italy
Tel: 39 2 2390/243/534; Fax: 2 70 600 462

Multidisciplinary association to increase awareness and spread knowledge of palliative care in Europe.

World Health Organization, Cancer and Palliative Care Unit, 1211 Geneva, Switzerland
Tel: 41 22 791 3477; Fax: 41 22 791 0746.

Assists the WHO's member states in the areas of cancer and palliative care; coordinates palliative care and cancer activities worldwide.

Appendix 2: Sources of Help Following Disasters

Civil Emergencies Secretariat, Home Office, Queen Anne's Gate, London SW1H 9AT, UK
Tel: 0171 273 3009; Fax: 0171 273 3900

Disaster and Emergency Reference Centre, Delft University of Technology, PO Box 5048-2600, GA Delft, The Netherlands

Disaster Planning and Limitation Unit, Department of Industrial Technology, University of Bradford, Bradford, West Yorkshire BD7 1DP, UK
Tel: 01274 733 466 ext. 8419

Disaster Research Center, University of Delaware, Newark, Delaware 19716, USA

Emergency Planning College, The Hawkhills, Easingwold, York YO6 3EG, UK

Emergency Services Branch, National Institutes of Health, Rockville, Maryland, USA

Federal Emergency Management Agency, 500 C Street, SW, Washington, DC 20472
Tel: 202 646 2500

Office of the United Nations Disaster Relief Coordinator, Palais des Nations, CH-1211, Geneva 10, Switzerland
Tel: +41 22 334 60 11

UK Disaster Research Network, Secretary Dr James Thompson, Academic Department of Psychiatry, University College and Middlesex School of Medicine, Grafton Street, London W1 E6AU, UK

References

Ainsworth, M. D. S. (1991) Attachments and other affectional bonds across the life cycle. In C. M. Parkes, J. Stevenson-Hinde and P. Marris (Eds) *Attachment Across the Life Cycle*. London: Routledge.

Allen, A. J. (1990) *Disaster: Planning for a Caring Response*, Part 1 and 2. London: HMSO.

Blueblond-Langner, M. (1978) *The Private Worlds of Dying Children*. Princeton: Princeton University Press.

Boswell, J. (1791) *The Life of Samuel Johnson LLD with his Observations and Conversations*. London: Griffin.

Bowlby, J. (1969) *Attachment and Loss. Vol. I, Attachment*. London: Hogarth Press.

British Association for Counselling (1993) *Code of Ethics and Practice for Counsellors*, 7th ed. Rugby: British Association for Counselling.

Couldrick, A. (1989) *Grief and Bereavement: Understanding Children*. Oxford: Sobell House.

Cruse (1995) *Bereavement Counselling: One-to-one and in Groups. The Best of Bereavement Care, No. 8*. Cruse: Bereavement Care, Cruse House, 126 Sheen Road, Richmond, Surrey TW9 1UR.

Danbury, H. (1996) *Bereavement Counselling Effectiveness: A client opinion study*. Aldershot: Avebury.

Doyle, D., Hanks, G. W. C. and MacDonald, N. (Eds) (1993) *Oxford Textbook of Palliative Medicine*. Oxford: Oxford University Press.

Dyregrov, A. (1991) *Grief in Children: A Handbook for Professionals*. London: Jessica Kingsley.

Eliot, T. S. (1954) The Hollow Men. *Selected Poems*. London: Faber.

Erikson, E.H. (1964) *Insight and Responsibility*. New York: Norton.

Franchino, L. (1994) *Bereavement Counselling and Supervision*. Four Training Videos, Cruse: Bereavement Care, Cruse House, 126 Sheen Road, Richmond, Surrey TW9 1UR.

Frank, A. W. (1991) *At the Will of the Body: Reflections on Illness*. Boston: Houghton Miflin.

Grollman, E. (1967) *Explaining Death to Children*. Boston: Beacon Press.

Hendriks, J. H., Black, D. and Kaplan, T. (1993) *When Father Kills Mother*. London: Routledge.

Hindmarsh, C. (1993) *On the Death of a Child*. Oxford: Radcliffe Medical Press.

Hodgkinson, P. E. and Stewart, M. (1991) *Coping with Catastrophe*. London: Routledge.

Kübler-Ross, E. (1970) *On Death and Dying*. London: Tavistock.

Markus, A. C., Parkes, C. M., Tomson, P. and Johnston, M. (1989) *Psychological Problems in General Practice*. Oxford: Oxford University Press.

Marris, P. (1982) Attachment and society. In C. M. Parkes and J. Stevenson-Hinde (Eds) *The Place of Attachment in Human Behaviour*. London: Tavistock; New York: Basic Books.

Miller, E. J. and Gwynne, G. V. (1972) *A Life Apart: A Pilot Study of Residential Institutions for the Physically Handicapped and the Young Chronic Sick*. London: Tavistock.

Parkes, C. M. (1979) Terminal care: evaluation of in-patient service at St Christopher's Hospice. II. Self-assessments of effects of the service on surviving spouses. *Postgraduate Medical Journal*, 55, 517.

Parkes, C. M. (1981) Evaluation of a bereavement service. *Journal of Preventive Psychiatry*, 1, 179–188.

Parkes, C. M. (1991) Planning for the aftermath. *Journal of the Royal Society of Medicine*, 84, 22–25.

Parkes, C. M. (1993) Psychiatric problems following bereavement by murder or manslaughter. *British Journal of Psychiatry*, 162, 49–54.

Parkes, C. M. (1996) *Bereavement: Studies of Grief in Adult Life*, 3rd ed. London: Tavistock.

Parkes, C. M., Laungani, P. and Young, W. (Eds) (1996) *Death and Bereavement Across Cultures*. London: Routledge.

Parkes, C. M. and Sills, C. (1994) Psychotherapy with the dying and the bereaved. In P. Clarkson and M. Pokorny (Eds) *The Handbook of Psychotherapy*. London: Routledge.

Parkes, C. M. and Weiss, R. S. (1983) *Recovery from Bereavement*. New York: Basic Books.

Raphael, B. (1986) *When Disaster Strikes*. New York: Basic Books.

Redmond, M. (1989) *Surviving when Someone you Know was Murdered*. Clearwater, Florida: Psychological Consultations and Education Services.

Relf, M. (1994) The effectiveness of volunteer bereavement support: reflections from the Sobell House Bereavement Study. Paper read at the *Fourth International Conference on Grief and Bereavement in Contemporary Society*, Stockholm, 12–16 June. Abstracts available from Swedish National Association for Mental Health, Stockholm.

Relf, M., Couldrick, A. and Barrie, H. (1986) *Grief and Bereavement*. Oxford: Sobell House Publications.

Rogers, C. (1951) *Client-Centred Therapy*. New York: Houghton-Mifflin.

Rogers, C. (1975) An unappreciated way of being. *Counselling Psychologist*, *21*, 95–103.

Seale, C. (1996) A comparison of hospice and hospital care. Unpublished report of work in progress.

Smith, S. C. and Tennels, M. (Eds) (1995) *Interventions with Bereaved Children*. London: Jessica Kingsley.

Stroebe, M. S., Schut, H. and van den Bout, J. (1994) The dual process model of bereavement. Paper read at the *Fourth International Conference on Grief and Bereavement in Contemporary Society*, Stockholm, 12–16 June. Abstracts available from Swedish National Association for Mental Health, Stockholm.

Twycross, R. (1994) *Pain Relief in Advanced Cancer*. Edinburgh: Churchill Livingstone.

Wertheimer, A. (1991) *A Special Scar: The Experiences of People Bereaved by Suicide*. London: Routledge.

Worden, J. W. (1982) *Grief Counselling and Grief Therapy*. London: Tavistock.

World Health Organization (1990) *Cancer Pain Relief and Palliative Care*. Technical Report Series 804. Geneva: World Health Organization.

Index